Building Catholic Higher Education

Building Catholic Higher Education

Unofficial Reflections from the University of Notre Dame

CHRISTIAN SMITH
with JOHN C. CAVADINI

CASCADE *Books* • Eugene, Oregon

BUILDING CATHOLIC HIGHER EDUCATION
Unofficial Reflections from the University of Notre Dame

Copyright © 2014 Christian Smith and John C. Cavadini. All rights reserved. Except for brief quotations in critical publications or reviews, no part of this book may be reproduced in any manner without prior written permission from the publisher. Write: Permissions, Wipf and Stock Publishers, 199 W. 8th Ave., Suite 3, Eugene, OR 97401.

Permission for the John Cavadini Appendix generously granted by *Commonweal* magazine, in which a version of it was previously published.

Cascade Books
An Imprint of Wipf and Stock Publishers
199 W. 8th Ave., Suite 3
Eugene, OR 97401

www.wipfandstock.com

ISBN 13: 978-1-62564-252-3

Cataloging-in-Publication data:

Smith, Christian.

Building Catholic higher education : unofficial reflections from the University of Notre Dame / Christian Smith with John C. Cavadini.

xvi + 112 p. ; 21 cm. —Includes bibliographical references.

ISBN 13: 978-1-62564-252-3

1. Catholic universities and colleges—United States. 2. Education, Higher—Aims and objectives. I. Title.

LC501 .S54 2014

Manufactured in the U.S.A.

This book is dedicated to Blessed Basil Moreau, CSC,
with gratitude.

Contents

Introduction

WHAT DOES IT MEAN to be a Catholic college or university today? And how can a Catholic mission be realized, given all the constraints and pressures in the real world of contemporary higher education? Catholic higher education has a long and venerable history in the West and in the United States. Yet for the past half-century, Catholic colleges and universities in the United States, at least, have struggled to enhance the quality and breadth of their education while remaining meaningfully and faithfully Catholic.

Many Catholic educational institutions have found that efforts to become more mainstream, to open up to the larger world of higher education, and to increase the quality of their instruction have had the unintended consequence of sidelining or diluting their Catholic character and identity. The forces of secularization have been and remain very powerful. Other Catholic colleges and universities find that attempts to maintain or foster seriously Catholic environments, curricula, and school culture easily lead to an insular, defensive, or sectarian posture that does not embody the best of the Catholic tradition. The forces of isolation and narrowness are also very powerful. So how can Catholic colleges and universities proceed to build themselves in ways that are educationally engaged and excellent, *and* authentically Catholic at the same time?

This short book seeks to enter already vibrant discussions of such matters, offering some very specific proposals from a very particular perspective.[1] My purpose in writing from a position of great specificity, to be sure, is to contribute to broad discussions. I am an academic scholar—a sociologist—not a university administrator, educational theorist, or certified expert on Catholic higher education. Most of my thoughts that follow in this book were formed during the course of my work at one particular Catholic university, the University of Notre Dame. In fact, much of what I have to say below has been developed with Notre Dame acting as a kind of sounding board.

In the following chapters, my own university serves as one concrete case in relation to which I develop a number of ideas about Catholic higher education—with the larger purpose of speaking to situations and people well beyond Notre Dame. The full scope of the questions and debates I address, therefore, are national and perhaps global. But I address those questions and debates through the lens of the particular case I know best, the University of Notre

1. For examples of the ongoing discussion, see Melanie M. Morey and John J. Piderit, *Catholic Higher Education: A Culture in Crisis* (Oxford: Oxford University Press, 2010); John Richard Wilcox, Jennifer Anne Lindholm, and Suzanne Dale Wilcox, *Revisioning Mission: The Future of Catholic Higher Education* (North Charleston, SC: CreateSpace, 2013); and Anne Hendershott, *Status Envy: The Politics of Catholic Higher Education* (New Brunswick, NJ: Transaction, 2009). Other parts of this literature focus on "practical" ways to change teaching and other practices in Catholic colleges and universities—for example, Thomas P. Rausch, *Educating for Faith and Justice: Catholic Higher Education Today* (Collegeville, MN: Liturgical, 2010), and John J. Piderit and Melanie M. Morey, *Teaching the Tradition: Catholic Themes in Academic Disciplines* (Oxford: Oxford University Press, 2012).

Dame. I do not mean thereby to suggest that Notre Dame is the paragon of all Catholic higher education, or that what might be good and right for Notre Dame must be good and right for everyone else, or anything of the sort. But I do believe that the working out of all these questions must be highly situated, and the answers that each local educational community arrives at must be appropriate for their individual circumstances and conditions. Therefore, I believe it good to wrestle with answers while referring to certain situated contexts. And my own context is Notre Dame. Nearly everything I write below, then, is worked out in engagement with the particular situation in which Notre Dame finds itself—a situation that, in my view, is extremely promising and exciting, but also challenging and in some ways precarious.

At the same time, however, I want to be very clear: this book is not only targeting people at Notre Dame. I wish through it to enter the larger discussions taking place around the United States and beyond about the nature, problems, and necessities of an authentically Catholic higher education. I will, in my writing, be engaging issues focused on Notre Dame. But I hope that readers not associated with Notre Dame can transpose what I say to engage their own Catholic college or university situations. I trust readers to do that kind of translation, to take my ideas away from my particular context and apply them to theirs.

What I mean by "authentic" Catholic higher education will become clearer below. Suffice it for now to say that it contrasts with colleges and universities that are Catholic in "heritage" only—that is, essentially secular schools that happen to be located in what were historically and now remain vaguely Catholic settings. Achieving that "heritage Catholic" outcome is easy, and probably the default outcome for Catholic institutions, given the forces at work in

American higher education today. What I instead want to consider here is the much harder question of what it means and what it takes to build and sustain robustly *Catholic* colleges and universities, in which the Catholic Church's faith and tradition continue to shape all aspects of academic life.

That may sound like a comprehensive agenda, and in a way it is, at least in its ultimate vision. On the other hand, this book's contribution to discussions about Catholic higher education is quite modest. Readers will find that I wish to contribute only a handful of key points to the discussions and debates. Some of what is most important, to my mind, actually concerns attitude and perspective. Still, those who care about Catholic higher education may find my ideas valuable and worth considering. I do not pretend to have anything like *the* answer or a comprehensive vision or program. The questions at hand are much too complex and arduous for any such thing. We need to move forward one contribution and conversation at a time. Happily, then, since my contribution to those conversations is fairly modest, this book is short and (I hope) sweet. It should be a quick and easy read that, I trust, proves stimulating and fruitful beyond its length.

It is very important for me to be clear, too, that *nothing in this book*—besides the official statements and documents that I quote in chapter 1—*represents the University of Notre Dame in any authorized, endorsed, or official capacity.* Nobody at Notre Dame asked me to write this book (if anything, there are probably some souls there who will wish I had not written it). Nobody has sanctioned its publication or put Notre Dame's seal of approval on it. I speak here only as one scholar reflecting on the history, experience, engagements, conflicts, and future of a particular university. I have a real stake in Notre Dame. But Notre Dame has not invested anything in this book. So if readers disagree

with or are unhappy about what I say, they have no reason to blame my leaders or colleagues (except, again, for
the official Notre Dame statements and documents that I
quote below)—they have enough difficulties and problems
of their own to take care of without having to answer for
those I create. I take full personal responsibility for what
follows, so all questions, doubts, and criticisms about this
book should be directed to me.

The essence of what I have to say in the chapters that
follow is this. Catholic colleges and universities need to
develop, articulate, explain, and promote clear and compelling visions of what it means in their institutions to be engaged in the task of Catholic higher education. Distinctive
visions that come from committed leaders are always the
place to start. Trying to work with or hide behind platitudes
and vapid sound bites is a recipe for failure. Institutional
leaders need to be explicit and unapologetic about their
Catholic mission. They must be ready to lead in alternative
directions within a sector of society that is now in some
confusion and disarray, rather than to follow the crowd.

Then, educators must spell out in concrete terms the
assumptions behind and implications following their visions. All too often, Catholic college and university leaders
leave Catholic mission-talk dangling at high altitudes of
generalities and clichés. That opens the door for confusion,
disagreement, and conflict among and between faculty and
administrators (and trustees and financial donors and parents and students) about what the institution is really trying
to accomplish and how it is attempting to do so. Trying to
please nearly everyone is impossible. It cannot and does
not work. More fair to everyone is to be as straightforward
and specific as possible about what the Catholic mission is,
what it concretely entails, and how the college or university
intends to realize it.

Next, I suggest, it is necessary to make clear to faculty, administrators, and staff who are not Catholic and who do not understand, or who cannot for various reasons directly support, the Catholic mission how they can nonetheless tacitly, passively, or indirectly support the Catholic mission in good conscience, instead of being forced to take marginal or dissenting positions. Most good Catholic mission statements—such as, in my view, that of the University of Notre Dame—explicitly welcome and value faculty, administrators, and staff who are not Catholic and even not mission-boosters, precisely because of the Catholic commitments that animate their institutional visions. Alternative perspectives and voices, in the right amounts and expressed in the right ways, are much-needed in institutions of Catholic inquiry and higher learning. But everyone needs to understand the bigger picture of how such perspectives can and should contribute to the shared but diverse pursuit of the larger Catholic mission. That can be done well—though often is not, which leads to troubles.

I then discuss how the Catholic commitment of a college or university might and, I think, should shape what it means to do social science at that institution. As a sociologist, I find my place among the social sciences. What could it mean to be a faculty member in the social sciences in a way that advances a school's Catholic mission? I strongly suspect that many faculty who have never been exposed to positive visions and practices of faith-based inquiry, scholarship, and teaching can readily conjure up in their minds negative and repellent images of how Catholicism might influence their academic work. No doubt more than a few hear "Catholic education" and think of inquisitions, lists of banned books, interference with academic freedom, employment discrimination, or worse. Others may simply sit in puzzlement, having no clue what *Catholic* education could mean at this level of schooling. If Catholic colleges and universities are to achieve their distinctive missions, they will have to find, develop, and promote fruitful means of bringing the Catholic faith to bear on their intellectual work. That is possible not only in the humanities, but also, I am sure, in the social sciences.

Finally, I attempt to parse out some of the sociological dynamics at work that influence the pursuit of the multiple goals that good Catholic mission statements usually include. Many institutions of Catholic higher education seek to combine excellence in undergraduate education with maintaining a serious Catholic identity, character, and mission. That is no easy task. Each of those is difficult alone; to combine them is much harder. Yet other Catholic colleges and universities—including my own University of Notre Dame—not only attempt that task, but also add a third, even more difficult goal: to engage in the highest quality original research, scholarship, and publishing in the sciences and humanities in an attempt to become a great research university. Realizing these three goals together is nearly impossible, though I refuse to say absolutely hopeless. The more everyone understands the many competing sociological and organizational forces, dynamics, and tendencies that make achieving them so difficult, the more possible it may become to realize these three goals—or at least to more effectively and efficiently attempt to achieve them.

I include after my chapters an Appendix written by my friend and colleague, Dr. John C. Cavadini, professor of theology, former long-time chair of the Department of Theology at Notre Dame, and Director of Notre Dame's Institute for Church Life. The Appendix is titled "The Role of Theology in a Catholic University." I believe it complements my chapters nicely by articulating a compelling vision and rationale for developing great departments of theology, as distinct from religious studies, at Catholic colleges and universities.

By the time readers have finished this short book, I hope that they will not only be better acquainted with some of the challenges and opportunities that are unfolding at the University of Notre Dame. They will also, I hope, have gained some new insights to bring to their own particular settings of higher education (if they are not "Domers"), which will help them approach the critical issue of building and sustaining faithfully Catholic colleges and universities in the United States and beyond. If my modest analyses and proposals can further that end, I will be gratified.

1

Lofty Visions

EVERY SUCCESSFUL INSTITUTION NEEDS a clear and compelling vision of its mission, which its leadership must continually articulate, explain, and promote. Such a vision is particularly important for institutions that are intentionally attempting to do something countercultural. "Without a vision, the people perish," wisely tells the ancient proverb. In the world of higher education today, Catholic colleges and universities that aim to be more than mere "secular institutions of learning in religious settings" especially need clear and compelling visions for their commitments to Catholic education. Everyone involved—administrators, trustees, faculty, students, parents, financial supporters, friends, and alumni—must know the mission and the institution's general approach to achieving it.

The sociological forces at work to undermine the integrity of Catholic higher education, to secularize Catholic colleges and universities, to force them to conform to purposes, standards, and programs that are often at odds with Catholic education are legion and immensely powerful. To resist them effectively without falling into a defensive, sectarian posture, which would be very un-Catholic, is a Herculean task—yet one that must be accomplished if Catholic colleges and universities are to be true to their histories, identities, and highest callings. First and foremost, if their missions are to be realized, Catholic colleges and universities must develop and advance clear and compelling statements of vision and mission.

Many Catholic colleges and universities do express strong mission statements. Among them is the University of Notre Dame, where I am privileged to work. In this brief chapter, I explore some of the key institutional statements of Catholic mission and vision that provide direction at Notre Dame. The University of Notre Dame has committed itself to a particular goal, in the words of President John Jenkins, of "becoming a preeminent research university with a distinctive Catholic mission and an unsurpassed undergraduate education." That mission, according to Notre Dame's "Vision and Goals" statement, entails the responsibility to "ensure that the University's Catholic character informs all its endeavors." The president, the provost, the board of trustees, and other major officers of Notre Dame are invested in and committed to achieving this mission. That is a necessary condition for a school like Notre Dame that seeks to have the Catholicity of its character significantly shape its work as a university.

Notre Dame pursues this mission in a variety of ways. But central among them is *building a faculty that supports and advances its mission*. A number of excellent statements and documents focused in part or entirely on the importance and character of Notre Dame's faculty for achieving its Catholic mission include "Notre Dame, Its Mission, Its Faculty" by President John Jenkins and Provost Thomas Burish (2008), the 2005 Inaugural Address by President

John Jenkins, the university's mission statement, a number of faculty addresses by President John Jenkins (2006–2011), and "The University of Notre Dame's catholic and Catholic Future: Professors, Teachers, and Scholarship" by Father Robert Sullivan (2008). Let us examine selections from these documents to see what I would argue are exemplary statements on Catholic higher education, and especially their emphasis on the role of faculty in that mission. I emphasize crucial phrases and sentences in italics, which are not part of the original documents.

MISSION STATEMENT OF THE UNIVERSITY OF NOTRE DAME[1]

The University of Notre Dame, declares its mission statement, is "a place of teaching and research, of scholarship and publication, of service and community. These components *flow from three characteristics of Roman Catholicism* that image Jesus Christ, his Gospel, and his Spirit. . . . A Catholic university draws its basic inspiration from Jesus Christ as the source of wisdom and from the conviction that in him all things can be brought to their completion. As a Catholic university, Notre Dame wishes to contribute to this educational mission."

That is a strong opening statement on behalf of the university's Catholic character and purpose. It continues: "The intellectual interchange essential to a university requires, and is enriched by, the presence and voices of diverse scholars and students. The Catholic identity of the University *depends upon, and is nurtured by, the continuing presence of a predominant number of Catholic intellectuals. This ideal has been consistently maintained by the University*

1. Online: http://nd.edu/aboutnd/mission-statement/.

leadership throughout its history. What the University asks of *all* its scholars and students, however, is not a particular creedal affiliation, but a *respect for the objectives of Notre Dame and a willingness to enter into the conversation that gives it life and character.*" Not all faculty at Notre Dame realize it, but the most important statement of the University's mission places great responsibility and expectations upon *all* of its faculty to understand and engage in its Catholic mission.

More: "Notre Dame's character as a Catholic academic community presupposes that no genuine search for the truth in the human or the cosmic order is alien to the life of faith. The University *welcomes all areas of scholarly activity* as consonant with its mission, *subject to appropriate critical refinement.* There is, however, *a special obligation and opportunity, specifically as a Catholic university, to pursue the religious dimensions of all human learning.* Only thus can Catholic intellectual life in all disciplines be animated and fostered and a proper community of scholarly religious discourse be established. In all dimensions of the University, Notre Dame pursues its objectives through the formation of an authentic human community graced by the Spirit of Christ." Notre Dame's mission statement thus leaves no doubt about the centrality of its Catholic commitments, identity, and educational goals.

STATUTES OF THE UNIVERSITY[2]

Notre Dame's statutes reinforce the same point: "*The essential character of the University as a Catholic institution of higher learning shall at all times be maintained,* it being the stated intention and desire of the present Fellows of the

2. Online: http://facultyhandbook.nd.edu/assets/41092/statutes_ of_the_university_april.29.2011.pdf, section V.(e).

University *that the University shall retain in perpetuity its identity as such an institution."*

"NOTRE DAME, ITS MISSION, ITS FACULTY"[3]

The Reverend John I. Jenkins, CSC, and Thomas G. Burish, the current president and provost of Notre Dame, respectively, have cogently developed what the Catholic mission of Notre Dame means for its faculty. They write:

> Universities are among the most important institutions of any society. They exercise a formative role as centers of teaching, learning, and research, with excellence at all levels as their goal. Originally, religion informed the structures, people, and practices of the university. Over time, most universities became secular centers that abstracted learning from the religious dimension of the human experience. The University of Notre Dame, however, continues to spring forth from the Catholic mission that created it.
>
> [We seek] to articulate the University's expectations of *how its faculty contribute and will contribute to realizing* its contemporary academic ambition of being a truly *preeminent and truly Catholic* university. The University of Notre Dame flourishes because of the academic achievements of men and women of faith and all seekers of truth: *faculty members, both Catholic and those of other faith traditions*, have supported and strengthened its Catholic mission; generations of students have received an education of body, mind, and spirit; and learning in service of

3. Online: http://provost.nd.edu/assets/4180/ndmissionand-faculty.pdf.

> social justice and human solidarity has thrived. As a vibrant, *religiously-inspired university*, Notre Dame aims to achieve academic preeminence in both teaching undergraduates and in graduate education and research. Because Notre Dame is committed to attaining greater academic *excellence as a Catholic university, fully realizing its religious character and mission is imperative.*

Very little ambiguity there.

They continue, writing about the education of students: "'Education,' said Blessed Basil Moreau, CSC, the founder of the Holy Cross Order, 'is the art of bringing a young person to completeness.' Notre Dame is committed to the flourishing of the *whole* person—intellectual, physical, moral, and *spiritual*. Teaching and learning here seek to foster in students the disciplined habits of mind, body, and spirit that characterize educated, skilled, generous, free human beings. Notre Dame wants to educate and inspire its students to be moral citizens within their communities and the larger world, to use their talents to the best of their ability, and to develop the generous sensibilities needed to relieve injustice, oppression, and poverty in all of their manifestations."

This, they then make clear, requires bringing the Catholic faith to bear on all of the intellectual work of the university. Writing about "The Fundamental Dialogue Between Faith and Reason," they argue:

> Essential to Notre Dame's mission is its *commitment to sustaining a dialogue between faith and reason across the disciplines.*[4] The conviction that

---

4. The language of "dialogue of faith and reason" works as long as everyone recognizes that the Catholic faith is reasonable and that reason is always based on some presupposed faith commitments.

there is ultimately no conflict between the truths of faith and those discovered by reason underlies our work as a Catholic university. Indeed, *the discoveries of reason enhance our understanding of faith, just as faith enhances our understanding of what reason discovers. Within the academy today, there exists widespread incomprehension of—even hostility toward—the conviction that religious and theological perspectives can speak to and enrich reasoned analysis. The resulting vacuum provides the University of Notre Dame with an opportunity—some might say the responsibility—*to even more strongly support the *efforts of its students and faculty to explore the intersections between faith and reason, pursuing both as mutually reinforcing rather than mutually exclusive.*

In order to achieve this difficult but critical goal, and *consistent with the Catholic intellectual tradition,* Notre Dame must remain committed to *free inquiry and open discussion, always informed by Catholic thought, of all legitimate achievements* in the arts, humanities, sciences, professions, and every other area of human scholarship and creativity. Questions concerning faith and reason, religion and discovery, the ethical dimensions of human life and works, and the integration of knowledge can arise in many venues, including the classroom, informal conversations between faculty and students, research and creative arts, and deliberations in departmental meetings or in committee discussions. Teaching and learning occur in countless ways in every university. At Notre Dame, the academic enterprise contains numerous opportunities for a fruitful dialogue between faith and reason.

Very sharp, very clear.

What then is the role of the *faculty*?

> Notre Dame . . . continues to embrace the challenge of being and becoming a preeminent research university, committed to educating its students, and *truly Catholic*. In *innumerable and essential ways, all faculty members at the University contribute to realizing this vision, each of them able to contribute uniquely out of his or her own beliefs, experiences, expertise, and talents. Working together, all faculty members at Notre Dame must ensure that an ever-wider range of scholarly interests, cultural heritages, social backgrounds, and viewpoints are present and thriving at the University.*
>
> The characteristics of universities that set them apart from other types of institutions are educational. For Notre Dame to maintain its commitment to being a Catholic university and not simply a Catholic institution in a broader sense, *the educational life of the university must be richly and diversely Catholic*. Faculty members are the core of every university's academic community, sustaining and directing the intellectual dialogue that occurs within this community.
>
> Engaged with all faculty in a common pursuit of truth, Catholic faculty bring to their teaching and research a faith commitment and an intellectual formation that enable them to relate issues in their respective disciplines to the beliefs, practices, and unresolved questions in the Catholic tradition. Along with their primary responsibility of providing the highest level of research and instruction, *Catholic faculty members also contribute to the holistic education of their students and the cultivation of their faith. Providing living examples of the legitimate*

diversity of adult Catholicism for their Catholic students, Catholic faculty offer counsel, engage in conversations relevant to their faith, and help students develop a faith that is informed, mature, and reflective. Catholic faculty members also have a special responsibility to explore the possible relationship of their Catholic faith with their own research and teaching, as well as to promote a more holistic form of education, in their informal interactions with other faculty and students. To fulfill Notre Dame's commitment to be such a Catholic educational community, the University seeks, in the words of its mission statement, "*the continuing presence of a predominant number of Catholic intellectuals.*"

These ideas I consider a model for Catholic higher education and the particular demands and opportunities it places before faculty.

Jenkins and Burish continue:

The University *also needs the contributions of faculty members of other faiths.* For Notre Dame to be truly Catholic, it *must be truly catholic,* home to the rich diversity of human thought, experience, and belief. Faculty members of other faith traditions enrich Notre Dame by sharing both their academic expertise and accomplishments, and their diverse perspectives. Such faculty members also provide examples of lived faith and exhibit the virtues that Notre Dame wants to instill in its students. They can foster in them a respect for other religious traditions and a commitment to ecumenical and interreligious dialogue, both of which are now critically needed in the world and essential to the success of a genuinely Catholic and catholic university.

In addition, *all seekers of truth are vitally important to the furtherance of the dialogue between faith and reason*, a foundational aspect of Notre Dame's academic mission. Such faculty members enrich, broaden, and advance the conversation between faith and reason so that this dialogue is truly inclusive and complete rather than a self-deceptive and narrow monologue. Thus faculty members of diverse faiths and all seekers of truth are indispensable in multiple ways to achieving the goals and fulfilling the mission of the University of Notre Dame. *Different faculty members will make different contributions. Every faculty member is likely to make varied contributions at various points in her or his career.* It is through these combined, diverse contributions that academic excellence will be achieved, *a continuing dialogue between faith and reason will be sustained*, and the development of the whole person—intellectual, physical, moral, and spiritual—will flourish.

Lofty visions, indeed.

They conclude: "Notre Dame aspires to be a preeminent research university, with a commitment to the complete education of its students, and *a distinctive and defining Catholic identity, character, and mission.* Our unique educational aspiration demands that we remain true to our heritage and mission by *combining the best of the secular and the religious traditions*, the highest level of inquiry and ethical reflection, and the commitment to educating and enriching the whole person. *The contributions of all faculty members to the University's mission are at once informed by their unique beliefs, talents, experiences, and expertise and vitally important to Notre Dame's academic achievement and Catholic character.* Only if Notre Dame is home to a community of scholars committed to educational excellence and the pursuit of truth in all of its manifestations, will it be true to its history and realize its aspirations for the future."

The vision here is admirably clear and, for many of us, compelling. Faculty working at the University of Notre Dame have no reason not to understand the very particular mission of the university and the distinctive claims it places upon them.

THE REVEREND JOHN I. JENKINS'S INAUGURAL ADDRESS[5]

On September 23, 2005, Notre Dame inaugurated a new president in the person of Rev. John I. Jenkins. The address he delivered at that occasion—excerpts of which I include below—contributes powerfully to the kind of mission statements we are exploring here, and is worth reviewing in some depth. "Notre Dame," Rev. Jenkins said, "is *a distinctively Catholic university* that strives to be among the preeminent universities in the world."

> What is the role of a Catholic university? Pope John Paul II once wrote that our proper activity is (and I quote): "Learning to think rigorously, so as to act rightly and to serve humanity better." The duty is timeless, yet its challenge is new in each age, and particularly pressing in this age. The *struggle to be a great Catholic university in a world that has become both increasingly secular and more radically religious* has placed Notre Dame in a *unique position* at the heart of the most complex issues facing our society. We have not just an opportunity, but *a duty* to think and speak and act in ways that will guide, inspire,

5. Online: http://inauguration.nd.edu/ceremonies/inaugural_address.shtml.

and heal—not just for the followers of the Catholic faith, but for all our neighbors in the nation and the world.

The world needs a great university that can address *issues of faith with reverence and respect* while still subjecting religion to intellectually rigorous, critical discussion. The world needs a university that not only contributes to scientific breakthroughs, but can address the *ethical implications* of scientific advances *by drawing on an ancient moral and spiritual tradition.* The world needs a university—grounded in a commitment to love one's neighbor—to debate how we in prosperous societies will respond to the grinding and dehumanizing poverty in which so much of the world lives. The world needs a university that graduates men and women who are not only capable and knowledgeable, but who accept their responsibility to serve others— especially those in greatest need. *The Catholic Church needs a university whose scholars can help pass on its intellectual tradition,* even as they address the challenges and the opportunities the Church faces in this century.

There are certainly other truly great universities in this country. Many of them began as religious, faith-inspired institutions, but nearly all have left that founding character behind. One finds among them a disconnect between the academic enterprise and an over-arching religious and moral framework that orients academic activity and defines a good human life. *My presidency will be driven by a whole-hearted commitment to uniting and integrating these two indispensable and wholly compatible strands of higher learning: academic excellence and religious faith. Building on our tradition as a Catholic university,* and determined to be counted among the preeminent universities in this country, *Notre Dame will provide an alternative for the twenty-first century*—a place of higher learning that plays host to world-changing teaching and research, but where technical knowledge does not outrun moral wisdom, where the goal of education is to help students live a good human life, where *our restless quest to understand the world not only lives in harmony with faith but is strengthened by it.*

We seek worldly knowledge, confident that the world exhibits coherence that reflects a Creator. We will train the intellects of our students, cultivate their faith and instill the virtues necessary for living a good life. We will strive to build a community generous to those in need and responsive to the demands of justice—strengthened by grace and guided by the command to love God and neighbor. *This is no easy mission.* But its difficulty is not our concern; *we did not create the mission, and we cannot change it.* The word "mission" derives from the Latin root *missus*—which means "sent." *We have been sent—to seek God,* study the world, and serve humanity. If we are clear in our purpose, we will excel in our ideals. This will be my priority and my passion as President of Notre Dame.

If we are looking for a clear and compelling vision for Catholic higher education, I believe we have one here.

Jenkins continues to explain:

> *The Catholic tradition insists on the unity of all knowledge. Truth is one.* Knowledge in every branch of inquiry is intrinsically valuable, and scholars in diverse disciplines pursue the same truth. Truths found in physics and biology do relate to those found in art, literature, and

philosophy, and our common pursuit of truth must include conversations across disciplines. The *Catholic tradition resists the fragmentation of knowledge; it insists on the essential unity of a university.* . . .Our *faith inspires our use of reason,* and *reason sharpens our understanding of faith.* Together, they both serve our *search for truth. We cannot legitimately claim to be a Catholic university if we do not affirm the central truths of divine revelation from Scripture and tradition.* As Augustine put it, "We see by the radiance of a light that's not our own."

Yet it would be a mistake to suppose that revealed truths provide us with a synthetic understanding of the world. For this reason, Pope John Paul II, in his encyclical *Fides et Ratio*, said there is no Catholic philosophy—no philosophy that the Church canonizes as its own. Similarly, there is no Catholic biology, or psychology, or political science. A Catholic university rejects a faith that trumps all claims of reason, and *rejects a rationalism that pre-empts all claims of faith.* Instead, *a Catholic university is a place where scholarly inquiry based on reason engages a theological tradition grounded in revelation.* Such a conversation between reason and revelation *may challenge some assertions of reasoned inquiry*, but it just as well challenges a complacent and false understanding of faith. The presence of such a conversation enriches a university, and *advances the search for truth.*

President Jenkins's helpful elaboration resumes:

During my presidency, we will give fresh emphasis to the *distinctive* strengths of Notre Dame, and we will build on these strengths as we move toward a preeminent position among the world's universities. . . . *Our research must not be separate from our Catholic mission,* but must draw strength from it and contribute to it. In areas where we have attained excellence, there is often a connection with that mission. *Every department, college, and institute must,* wherever possible, find dimensions of their *research agenda that reflect our Catholic character and values.*

At a time when a national debate on the relationship between science and religion has emerged, when we're pressed for an answer to the poverty and hopelessness in so many lands, when our environment is threatened, and technology is changing our lives in complex ways, Notre Dame must be the university *that combines the highest level of disciplinary expertise with the resources of its moral and religious tradition.* We *step onto controversial ground here. Yet if we at Notre Dame do not address these issues, whose voice will fill the void?* We must take on the social, moral, and economic issues where we can make a distinctive contribution. . . .

We must also *recognize and affirm the value of religious diversity at Notre Dame.* Within our community are Protestant and Orthodox Christians, Jews, Muslims, Hindus, Buddhists, and those of other religious traditions and no religious tradition. As we affirm the Catholic identity of Notre Dame, we *acknowledge and embrace the many non-Catholics who are deeply committed to this university and its principles,* and who labor so hard on its behalf. If we were *exclusively Catholic, we would be less catholic—* less broad, less universal, with fewer opportunities to enrich our dialogue and test our ideas with those who share many of our values, but not all of our views.

Notre Dame is different. Combining religious faith and academic excellence is not widely emulated or even admired among the opinion-makers in higher education. Yet, in this age especially, *we at Notre Dame must have the courage to be who we are. If we are afraid to be different from the world, how can we make a difference in the world?* As we stand at the start of the twenty-first century, there are no footprints ahead to show the way. *Yet our difference is not a detriment. It is an asset that will make our contribution more distinctive,* more exemplary, more valuable. We welcome the challenge. . . .

With respect and gratitude for all who embraced Notre Dame's mission in earlier times, let us rise up and embrace the mission for our time: to build a Notre Dame that is bigger and better than ever—*a great Catholic university* for the twenty-first century, one of the preeminent research institutions in the world, a center for learning *whose intellectual and religious traditions converge* to make it a healing, unifying, enlightening force for a world deeply in need. *This is our goal. Let no one ever again say that we dreamed too small.*

PRESIDENT JOHN I. JENKINS'S 2006 ANNUAL ADDRESS TO THE FACULTY[6]

Since delivering his inaugural address in 2005, President Jenkins has every year reinforced his message about Notre Dame's Catholic mission to faculty in his annual faculty

---

6. Online: http://president.nd.edu/writings-addresses/2006-addresses/president-s-annual-address-to-the-faculty/.

addresses. Excerpts from his 2006 faculty address, for example, told Notre Dame faculty this:

> We are *a distinctively Catholic university* that strives to be among the preeminent universities in the world. We must therefore *recognize, cherish, and enhance the distinctive character of Notre Dame*, and, at the same time, we must strive to excel in teaching, learning, and research by the standards of truly great institutions of higher learning. These two challenges—promoting truly great teaching and scholarship while *preserving and enhancing our Catholic character—are my top priorities as President* of Notre Dame. . . .
>
> Our *Catholic character* . . . gives us *a special capacity to undertake a range of inquiries in matters of faith and morals*. Whether it is discussion of the doctrine of the Divine Trinity—the doctrine that God is Three Persons, Father, Son, and Holy Spirit—or an interreligious dialogue, or a forum on global health and our moral responsibilities, *we can, because of our religious character, easily hold conversations that cannot be readily held, or perhaps not held at all, at other universities*. We can do so because, while we are committed to reasoned inquiry, *we embrace convictions of faith*; while we are open to questioning, we *subscribe institutionally to a clear understanding of what a good human life is*, and we strive to help our students live such a life. . . .
>
> *Our distinctive character also presents us with challenges not faced by other universities.* Last year, as you know, we had a serious, rigorous discussion involving faculty, students, and many outside the University about what the policy of this University should be regarding campus events that may be at odds with our Catholic mission. . . .

The greater sense of community, the emphasis on ethics and morals, the special capacity to inquire into God, religion, and eternal truth—these are special *distinctions and advantages that come from our Catholic identity, but they don't come automatically, and they don't come without a corresponding commitment on our part. These advantages come only as we pursue the Catholic mission that distinguishes the work of the University, and sets us—in some ways—on a different course from most other universities.* I believe that there are at least three dimensions to that distinctive Catholic mission.

Very clear, very compelling. Jenkins continued with the faculty:

A third and final dimension of our Catholic mission is in our *commitment to serve the Catholic Church.* The University is incorporated under a group of Fellows, who are Trustees with a special responsibility for guarding the Catholic mission of the University, as well as the full Board of Trustees. Under this two-level Board, the University is autonomous in its governance, yet it recognizes that *part of its mission is to serve the Catholic Church.* Catholics believe that the Church is a community which finds its origin in Jesus Christ and his apostles, is enlivened by the Holy Spirit, and exists for the proclamation of the Gospel message and the sanctification of people. It is difficult to explain such a rich notion in a few words, but it means at least that, *for Catholics, the Church is the context in which Christian faith and culture, Christian identity, cease to be simply objects of speculation and controversy, and become human and concrete.* The Church is an institutional reality, but for Catholics it is also a theological and a mystical reality, the body of Christ living in time. Because *the living Church needs to think and reflect and remember, it relies for its intellectual sustenance on Catholic universities as places of teaching, learning, and inquiry.* There is, I believe, *no university in the world that is better able to serve the Church, and it is part of our mission to do so.*

We can succeed in advancing these aspects of the University's mission *only if we have, among our faculty, a critical number of devoted followers of the Catholic faith.* Such faculty members have a contribution to make in passing on the Church's moral and intellectual tradition, in reflecting on issues of religious belief, and in embracing, as Catholics, *a special vocation to serve their Church.* I am *not saying that such Catholics are better or smarter or more gifted in pursuing the specific academic aims of our University.* This is not the case, and it is not my claim. I am saying that *high numbers of Catholic faculty members who are active in the faith are indispensable to this University, if we are to be successful in fulfilling our mission. For this reason we have sought, and will continue to seek, a preponderance of faculty at the University who are Catholic.* Consequently, we must *remain vigilant about the percentage of new hires who are Catholic,* devise strategies to *attract superb Catholic scholars, and explain why we do so.*

At the same time, I want to say something that is obvious, but may perhaps need more emphasis: *faculty members who are not Catholic are indispensable to the life and success of Notre Dame*—in promoting scholarship, in building community, in provoking debate, in pushing for excellence, in ensuring diversity of perspectives. *Non-Catholic faculty do exceptional work in teaching, research, and administration. They make us a better university. They also make us a better Catholic university,* for they enrich our understanding of God, who is all-inclusive, and our conversations about faith. . . .

And our colleagues who neither embrace religion nor believe in God can help us enhance our dialogue with the significant number of the world's people who have no particular religious tradition. If Notre Dame is to be a force for understanding and healing in a fractured world, we must not only foster dialogue among people of different faiths, but also between *people who seek truth in God and religion and those who seek it elsewhere.* This is why I believe that *every member of our faculty, Catholic or not, can contribute to the religious mission of this University.* I am particularly grateful to and inspired by the many non-Catholics who take the mission of Notre Dame to heart and assist in it. . . .

The *challenge* for Notre Dame in coming years is *complex;* we *must preserve a unique and beloved heritage,* advance the University academically, and *fulfill in an even richer way our distinctive Catholic mission.* We cannot meet this challenge unless we *choose*—in all the many guises in which this choice will be offered—the *more ambitious, more challenging path over a safer, more comfortable, more familiar one.* If we choose the easier path, we can be a very fine, very beloved university that does significant good in society, but we will be a university that has retreated from its *chance to play a special role* in the world. If we choose the more difficult path, we will answer the call to play a critical role in serving the Church, the nation, and the world in the twenty-first century. I have made my choice, and I am asking you to join me. . . .

And do not console yourself that—if Notre
Dame chooses not to become a great Catholic
university for the twenty-first century—some
other institution will come forward to play
that role. *There are, indeed, many fine Catholic
institutions in the country and the world,* and it
serves our interest when any of them aspire to
academic excellence or embrace their Catholic
mission deeply. *Yet, in my view, there is no university in the country, or I believe in the world,
that combines, better than we do, our rich academic potential with a profound commitment to
Catholic mission.*

If any faculty anywhere were misled to believe that Notre
Dame was just another elite American university, Rev. Jenkins surely corrects their misunderstandings here.

PRESIDENT JOHN I. JENKINS'S 2007 ANNUAL ADDRESS TO THE FACULTY[7]

Notre Dame faculty who may have assumed that President
Jenkins's lofty talk about Catholic education in 2006 was
mere first-year window dressing found out differently in his
2007 faculty address, when he said,

To fulfill our mission, our distinctive Catholic
character should inform all endeavors of the
university, and no area is more important than
the intellectual life that is the heart of this community. We aspire to be a place in which religious
faith and spiritual values are not just respected,
but lived, explored, and cultivated, where research on issues of religious faith is conducted at

7. Online: http://president.nd.edu/writings-addresses/2007-
addresses/president-s-annual-address-to-the-faculty/.

the highest scholarly level, and *where a dialogue between faith and reason is present across the disciplines.*

It is *not necessary, of course, that every faculty member make issues of religious faith and spirituality an intellectual focus. It is, however, desirable that some do—and that all respect the value of such research at Notre Dame.* And because we are a Catholic university, I believe that *we must have a preponderance of Catholic faculty and scholars, those who have been spiritually formed in that tradition and who embrace it. This will continue to be an emphasis for us.* At the same time, I believe that *faculty of other religious traditions and no religious tradition enrich the intellectual life of this university and enrich it precisely as a Catholic university.* Notre Dame *must be a place for respectful, informed dialogue about matters of faith and spirituality, and we cannot be such a place without those who embrace other great religious traditions.* Moreover, we *must be a place where religious belief and unbelief are in dialogue,* and therefore we are *enriched by those who do not share religious faith, but are willing to engage in serious dialogue with those who do.*

PRESIDENT JOHN I. JENKINS'S ANNUAL ADDRESSES TO THE FACULTY, 2008–2011

The same message to faculty was delivered by the president year after year. For example, in 2008, Rev. Jenkins stated that, "Our central goals are to be unsurpassed in undergraduate education, to become a premier research university with a superb graduate program, and *to ensure that our Catholic character informs the university's activities in ways that enrich our intellectual, communal, and spiritual lives.* More succinctly put, *we strive to be a truly great, truly Catholic university. Pursuit of these ideals has been and will always remain at the heart of our efforts.*"[8]

In his 2009 faculty address, he noted, "I began this address by talking about *Notre Dame's distinctive role in higher education.* The heart of that distinctiveness is to strive to achieve three central goals which can sometimes be in tension—superb undergraduate education, preeminence in research, and *ensuring our Catholic mission informs all our endeavors.* Other great universities have recognized the tension between a commitment to research and to undergraduate education, and I am proud of the way you have continued to make the education of undergraduates a cornerstone as we strive to be even stronger in research. Our commitment to our Catholic mission creates its own set of challenges and tensions. Yet it is precisely because we hold these goals simultaneously that *we have such a special mission and play such a distinctive role.* And our achievements are due to the efforts of you and many others."[9]

In 2010, he reiterated: "The *struggle to be a great Catholic research university in a world that has become both increasingly secular and more radically religious has placed Notre Dame in a unique position* at the heart of the most complex issues facing our society. A glance at newspaper headlines shows that religious strife can complicate efforts to spread peace around the world. . . . Notre Dame has lent, and must continue to lend, its voice to this discussion. We have *not just an opportunity, but a duty* to think and speak and act in ways that will guide, inspire, and heal. Building

8. Online: http://president.nd.edu/writings-addresses/2008-addresses/president-s-annual-address-to-the-faculty/.

9. Online: http://president.nd.edu/writings-addresses/2009-addresses/president-s-annual-address-to-the-faculty/.

on our tradition, *Notre Dame will provide an alternative* for the twenty-first century—a place of higher learning that plays host to world-changing teaching and research, but where technical knowledge does not outrun moral wisdom, where the goal of education is to help students live a good human life, where *our restless quest to understand the world not only lives in harmony with faith but is bolstered by it*."[10]

And, again, in 2011, Father Jenkins insisted that "*Notre Dame's resources do have a sacred character that imposes duties upon each of us.* If for no other reason, *we owe it to the benefactors, parents, and those who have gone before us* to make the most of what we have received; we owe it to our students to give them the best education we can; and we owe it to the world to give it the benefits of our scholarship, research, and creative work. We ought to see these resources as '*sacred deposits' that we must use to serve the mission of Notre Dame* and make it even more powerfully a force that heals, unifies, and enlightens. The needs are urgent."[11]

The message to faculty from the top of the university, in short, has been clear, consistent, and strong. Notre Dame is a distinctively Catholic university in pursuit of a difficult

10. Online: http://president.nd.edu/writings-addresses/2010-addresses/president-s-annual-address-to-the-faculty/.

11. Online: http://president.nd.edu/writings-addresses/2011-addresses/president-s-annual-address-to-the-faculty/. The president's 2012 address to the faculty was unusual in focusing on a variety of very practical issues, but he nonetheless made sure to say that "Notre Dame has a prominent place in the Catholic Church nationally and internationally" and emphasized the need "to fashion a role for Notre Dame of genuine assistance to the Church" by organizing "to convene and lead world-wide dialogue that serves the Church and is relevant to the Catholic intellectual tradition" (http://president.nd.edu/writings-addresses/2012-addresses/presidents-annual-address-to-the-faculty/).

and challenging goal, and it needs its faculty to understand and support that.

"FORMATION OF THE AD HOC COMMITTEE ON RECRUITING OUTSTANDING CATHOLIC FACULTY"—LETTER FROM PROVOST TOM BURISH, FEBRUARY 5, 2007[12]

These lofty visions for Catholic higher education as expressed at the University of Notre Dame have not come from the president alone. Notre Dame's provost, Tom Burish, has also made clear in a variety of ways his commitment to Notre Dame's Catholic vision. One of those ways concerns the hiring of Catholic faculty, about which the provost wrote the following.

> *Attracting outstanding Catholic faculty is a stated and serious goal of Notre Dame,* but so too is recruiting, supporting, and promoting outstanding faculty from other traditions. Because of our recent history in faculty recruiting, I believe *the greatest immediate challenge is to recruit more outstanding Catholic faculty*—hence the current emphasis on it. . . . It [the committee] is charged with assessing four major issues associated with recruiting outstanding Catholic faculty: (1) the supply of suitably qualified Catholic faculty members; (2) the best practices for hiring Catholic faculty members; (3) a strategy for coordinating our various hiring processes for Catholic faculty with our broader faculty hiring goals;

12. Online: https://provost.nd.edu/assets/3872/burish_sapc_catholic_recruiting_letter_to_faculty.pdf; also see https://provost.nd.edu/for-current-faculty/past-initiatives/ad-hoc-committee-on-recruiting-outstanding-catholic-faculty/.

and (4) strategies to ensure a strong pipeline of Catholic faculty in the future. . . .

As you know, Notre Dame's mission statement affirms that *"the Catholic identity of the University depends upon, and is nurtured by, the continuing presence of a predominant number of Catholic intellectuals."* A forthcoming white paper seeks to explain the academic and strategic reasons for, and possible benefits of, our commitment to maintaining a predominant number of Catholic intellectuals. *Since Notre Dame began, there has always been a predominant number of Catholic faculty at the University.* The percentage of Catholic faculty, however, is in decline. . . . It is clear that without intelligently creative and systematic attention to this challenge, the overall percentage of faculty who are Catholic will likely drop below 50 percent in the near future. As a University, *we must be increasingly attentive to how we can recruit and retain outstanding Catholic faculty.* . . .

Our particular challenge is sustaining three demographic objectives [women, minorities, and Catholic faculty], rather than two, as is the case at most other peer institutions. Can we maintain these priorities simultaneously without compromising any of them? *I believe we can if we are willing* to use every strategy available to us and if we are *willing to devote significant resources to the effort.* I am committed, with your help, to doing everything we can to address meaningfully and strategically all our demographic priorities.

CONCLUSION

These statements and documents make absolutely clear where Notre Dame stands on the matter of Catholic mission and education.[13] That clarity is highly admirable and a huge asset to Notre Dame as it goes about pursing that distinctive mission. I would hope that these statements and documents might also serve as models for other Catholic colleges and universities attempting to sort out their own visions and missions.

At the same time, the authors of these statements and documents have been appropriately careful not to spell out in too much detail all of the assumptions and implications of their approach to faculty concerning its mission. Notre Dame's statements on the matter have aptly articulated its major principles and avoided enumerating specific rules. I am personally impressed by these many statements and documents, believing that they have gotten matters quite right.

13. Other documents relevant to this chapter's focus on visions for Catholic education include an "Ad Hoc Committee on Recruiting Outstanding Catholic Faculty: Report," Committee Report, September 18, 2007, https://www3.nd.edu/~provost/for-current-faculty/assets/report_of_the_ad_hoc_committee_on_recruiting_outstanding_catholic_faculty_final_committee_draft.pdf; "Ad Hoc Committee on Recruiting Outstanding Catholic Faculty: Status of Recommendations," Letter from Provost Tom Burish, August 28, 2008, https://provost.nd.edu/assets/33925/provostfacultyletter8.28.2008.pdf; and "Common Proposal [on Academic Freedom]," Common Proposal of Chairs of the College of Arts and Letters and Fr. Jenkins, April 5, 2006, http://president.nd.edu/communications/statements-on-academic-freedom/closing-statement/common-proposal/. For a statement committing Notre Dame to its Catholic mission before the John I. Jenkins era, see "Report: A Strategic Plan Notre Dame 2010: Fulfilling the Promise," published February 7, 2003, http://www.nd.edu/~stratgic/final/index.shtml.

Nevertheless, the more practical implications of constitutional and guiding statements like those above need to be elaborated elsewhere. They benefit from interpretive commentaries that seek to draw out their specific meaning and implications. Such commentaries may carry no formal authority. But they can help to frame constructive discussions about important matters. My purpose in what follows in this book is to offer one logical, faithful understanding of the practical implications of the statements and documents examined above.

CHAPTER APPENDIX

In addition to the many statements and documents examined above, one further document that has also been important at Notre Dame, even if it lacks some of the official status of statements from the president and provost, has been the paper "The University of Notre Dame's catholic and Catholic Future: Professors, Teaching, and Scholarship—A White Paper, 2008," authored by Rev. Robert Sullivan, Department of History and the Erasmus Institute, with the editorial assistance of Walton R. Collins, emeritus, Department of American Studies, University of Notre Dame.[14] I believe it is worth including here. Excerpts from it read as follows.

The vision of Notre Dame as a distinctively Catholic research university sharing in academic preeminence makes it *unusual, perhaps singular in one way.* There exists *no accessible model* for Notre Dame's project of becoming a preeminent research university by *growing the Catholicism of both its academic programs and its faculty.* To develop further as a comprehensive (or catholic) university, it must

14. Online: http://provost.nd.edu/assets/3686/sullivan_white_paper_abridged.pdf.

continue to grow its faculty academically, recruit and retain more women and minority professors, and *maintain
religious diversity and inclusiveness within the faculty.* The
American academy generally and properly shares those
as essential goals. *Only a few research universities here and
abroad, including Notre Dame, support the deeper and wider
development of the academic potential of the intellectual and
cultural resources of Catholicism.* Notre Dame, however, also
*seeks to advance as a Catholic university by recruiting and
retaining greater numbers of first-rate Catholic academics.*

It is *perhaps the University's biggest challenge.* For over
seventy-five years no preeminent American university has
noticed religion when hiring professors, except to discrimi-
nate against those who were not People Like Us—often
Jews. Today in some religiously affiliated colleges and universities, one form of exclusion or another usually shapes
projects of recruiting faculty to support the institutional
mission. Though legal, such a bias can prove ethically dubi-
ous and intellectually stifling, and it is inadmissible at Notre
Dame.

*Academics may reasonably view the University's com-
mitment to recruiting faculty to advance it as a Catholic
university with skepticism, embarrassment, dismay, or fear,*
as well as with interest and support—*mindless hostility* is a
case apart. Creating a distinctively Catholic, academically
preeminent university will *require candid, searching conversations involving professors* and administrators as well as
trustees and alumni; refining, where appropriate, the policy
in light of those conversations; framing a strategic plan to
implement the policy; *designing and managing tactics and
structures to assist the University's colleges and schools in
executing the policy*; and providing the resources to implement it. The success of those conversations depends on an

understanding of the unique situation and uncertain prospects of the contemporary university. . . .

Because the University of Notre Dame is *a Catholic academic community* of higher learning, *that long history of human education informs its mission and identity*. To the classical moral virtues (justice, fortitude, temperance, and prudence), Christianity added the religious virtues of faith, hope, and love. *Christianity's distinctive beliefs, ethics, and worship* were meant to infuse the usages that gave schools their ethos, and it in turn *imbued teachers with exemplary habits.* . . . *Notre Dame is pulled* on the one side by the research university's tendency to reduce education to discovering and transmitting knowledge, and on the other *by the Catholic goal* of providing human education. *The tension can be either creative or destructive* for the University, but it is *permanent.* History moves in only one direction. There is no going back to the future. Notre Dame's flourishing depends on strengthening its academic excellence and reputation, as well as its *distinctively Catholic ethos and appeal.* . . .

Notre Dame prizes the generous and necessary secular values esteemed at every responsible college. Additionally, its distinctive identity requires that it deepen the Catholic spiritual and ethical education that most of its undergraduates began at home, and even experiment with extending it to graduate students. Unlike secular institutions, Notre Dame properly aspires to "provide [such students] with *explicit advice about moral virtue" and religious faith and knowledge* as well. The University must articulate *what defines professors who can participate in fulfilling its "pastoral obligation" to Catholics* and other students who enroll here *expecting a Catholic ethos and human education. Otherwise, Notre Dame, though catholic, will cease to be distinctively Catholic and will thereby forfeit a mainstay of its academic appeal and its opportunity* to make a distinctive academic contribution. . . .

Notre Dame must continue *educating its Catholic undergraduates so that their Catholicism is not only hereditary and convivial but also informed by reasoned conviction and generous action.* If they come to the University from various Catholic neighborhoods, they must leave equipped to form Catholic and other religious and ethical networks, wherever they are. Only thus will our alumni be able to cooperate intelligently with Catholics and other persons of good will to promote social justice. . . . *Reclaiming Catholic intellectual and cultural resources for Catholicism is a task for academic specialists working in normal departments.* Along with Notre Dame's eminent Theology Department, the accomplished philosophers who work in sub-disciplines with Catholic implications are academically indispensable. Their departments continue to enjoy a formative role here, but *our Catholic academic project is now more extensive.*

The University already supports the research and creativity of many faculty members whose scholarship and art deepen the Catholic intellectual and cultural achievement. *Even more diverse Catholic scholarship is needed if the University is to fulfill its ambitious mission statement* by realizing its own "special obligation and opportunity, specifically as a Catholic university, to pursue the religious dimensions of all human learning . . . [so that] Catholic intellectual life in all disciplines [can] be animated and fostered and a proper community of scholarly religious discourse be established." Such scholarship and creativity are likely to be crucial for strengthening the social sciences, humanities, and arts at Notre Dame, even as the physical and biological sciences grow in importance. Such scholarship and creativity can also enable the University to gain a *distinct advantage within the larger academy. By engaging more fully major*

31

Catholic intellectual and cultural resources that scholarship has tended to secularize or neglect, the University can *play a more vital and visible role as a catholic university.*

For Notre Dame to specialize in, and even create, more academic subfields with a Catholic import *depends on the Catholic idea of tradition: It is not some intellectual and cultural dead hand, or the savoring of curious erudition, but today's intelligent engagement with and development of the past.* Because history flows on, any academic project that purports somehow to effect a Catholic "restoration" is at best fanciful. Propaganda and moralism never substitute for scholarship. Notre Dame's *Catholic academic enterprise presupposes creative, rigorous, and learned scholars who help to make the University a stronger presence in the academy and draw other talented academics here.* Many able graduate students choose Notre Dame because of our strengths in areas with an important Catholic or other religious component. Far from taking for granted our competitive advantage, we must retain and expand it by improving these strengths. . . . Notre Dame's capacity to support *additional and more sophisticated scholarship in Catholic cultural and intellectual resources* also *depends on the presence of an aggregation of faculty members, Catholic as well as other believers and nonbelievers, specialist and non-specialist alike, who value those resources, even when they do not study them.* . . .

A serious research university whose appeal is also distinctively Catholic must offer spiritual and moral education to its Catholic students, particularly to its undergraduates. That requires the academic resources of many disciplines—as well as a residential life that supports community, a sophisticated campus ministry, programs that enable social justice and social concern, and *an aggregation of Catholic faculty humanly available to their overwhelmingly Catholic students.* If the cultivation of a distinctive human education

distinguishes such a university from its secular counterparts,
like them it respects the fundamental academic protocols
in faculty recruitment, promotion, and research. In addition, such a university will support research and creativity
that investigate, express, or grow Catholic intellectual and
cultural resources. The merits of a particular achievement
invite academic scrutiny, and scholarly work on it must be
technically proficient. Such a university sees those achievements as informed by religious belief, accessible to us but
also open to eternity. Finally, *such a university's ethos will
feel different from that of its secular counterparts.* It will be
*populated by intellectually alert and honest people who ap-
preciate that faith and doubt are now correlative* [editorial
clarification: i.e., faith can be a matter of certitude but not
certainty]. Serious religions, including *Catholicism, cannot
therefore be patronized or ignored at such a university. In
turn, Catholic and other honest believers there can respect
and cooperate with honest doubters because they, too, understand doubt. . . .*

Because *the whole faculty, along with many others, is
responsible for sustaining this complex educational mission,*
the University seeks to recruit and retain professors for
whom teaching and scholarship are more than one more
career choice. And it has been largely successful. Many
Notre Dame faculty members foster in their students the
intellectual and ethical virtues that support the "disciplined
habits of mind, body, and spirit which characterize educated, skilled, and free human beings." The faculty's pursuit
of understanding and truth requires of them integrity, hard
work, the accurate and helpful use of language, and coop-
eration with and care for other people. The human education that the University seeks to offer depends on the deep
vision of humanity that infuses the faculty who exemplify
those virtues: yes, we are minds, but we are also bodies and

spirits. Notre Dame aspires, moreover, to build on those sacred habits in order to *offer its students a human education open to God's mysterious transcendence incarnated in us and in our world. Without the virtues of the whole faculty, the University must fail in its lofty aspiration.*

Sustaining such an ethos *requires a division of labor among the faculty*, with *Catholic professors sharing principal responsibility for the religious dimension of its overwhelmingly Catholic student body's human education.* The division informs perhaps the most contentious sentence in Notre Dame's mission statement: the "Catholic identity of the University depends upon, and is nurtured by, *the continuing presence of a predominant number of Catholic intellectuals."* That has been *the reality of Notre Dame from the beginning.* The official commitment has two purposes. First, it aims to make the University home for an aggregation of professors—female and male, lay and religious—that embodies, inside and outside the classroom, the *legitimate diversity of adult Catholicism for their Catholic students.* Second, the commitment aims to ensure that the faculty contains an aggregation of professors concerned with the "special obligation . . . to pursue the religious dimensions of all human learning . . . [so that] Catholic intellectual life in all disciplines [can] be animated and fostered and a proper community of scholarly religious discourse be established." *Absent sufficient numbers of Catholic professors, how can the University properly attend to a distinctively Catholic intellectual and cultural achievement? . . .*

History and demography make Catholics and other minorities generally allergic to exclusionary and discriminatory policies. That reality frames the theoretical and practical inclusiveness of Notre Dame's policy of recruiting faculty to support its mission. *The University imposes no religious test on its faculty* for hiring or promotion, and it actively enlists and promotes all qualified academics *who can contribute to its catholic—and in some cases Catholic—flourishing.* Notre Dame *does not elevate Catholic professors above their colleagues of other religions or none* but recruits them to serve students out of their own religious witness and, in some cases, Catholic learning. *All professors fully belong, and they can thrive here.* . . . Most Catholics are integrated into the American mainstream. *Preserving their identity* requires that they nurture excellent institutions that express their own particularity. Only thus will they be preserved from so completely integrating into the mainstream that they lose anything usefully *distinctive* to contribute to the nation's academic mosaic. . . .

To become a distinctively Catholic great university, *Notre Dame must widen and intensify the study and teaching of Catholicism's cultural and intellectual achievements beyond the disciplines of theology and philosophy.* . . . For a Catholic university to fulfill its responsibility of offering Catholic intellectual and cultural education, many of its *faculty must be able to teach students out of their own research in major cultural and intellectual expressions of Catholicism.* The richness of those resources can, moreover, academically strengthen some of Notre Dame's doctoral programs. . . . Because Notre Dame *rejected the prophecy that modernization entails secularization*, it is uniquely positioned to lead in discovering *how to reintroduce religion—and not just Catholicism—into the academy,* to lead in creating the twenty-first-century university. . . .

For Notre Dame to cultivate more fully the study of specifically Catholic intellectual and cultural resources *demands much imagining, planning, and executing.* The University must devote attention and resources to making an *even more original* contribution to American higher education, while accelerating the conventional academic trajectory that has so improved it. Many of Notre Dame's departments creatively deploy their human and other resources in *academic enterprises in which Catholicism matters, or can matter, and those departments are growing better. . . . Roman Catholicism tries to be respectful of all serious religions.* Because God makes the "dialogue of salvation" universally accessible, *the Church's "dialogue too should be as universal as we can make it,"* Pope Paul VI wrote in 1964. . . . Catholicism enjoys, however, a unique theological and spiritual kinship with other forms of Christianity, with Judaism, and with Islam. As religions worshiping the one God, they share and contest a religious idiom. The unique relationship imposes on *Catholics as Catholics a religious obligation of maintaining serious, learned conversations with the other Abrahamic religions.* If the University is to *pursue the religious dimensions of all human learning and build a proper community of scholarly religious discourse*, it must successfully recruit and retain professors who belong to other Christian churches and communities and study their distinctive achievements. Their learned participation is required for Notre Dame to fulfill the ecumenical imperative defined at the Second Vatican Council. For our Catholic undergraduates to be truly Catholic, they must know and understand their fellow Christians. . . .

Can Notre Dame's *effort to pioneer a new way in higher education* be made intelligible to the first-class academics whom it seeks to recruit, in light of their secular experience of the research university? If so, will they find the experiment inviting or off-putting? In the age of academic professionalism, is it practicable to *ask faculty who are not Catholic* and with good prospects elsewhere *not only to respect but also to support the University's distinctive Catholic ethos*? Can Notre Dame nurture an academic culture founded on a shared sense of University citizenship among a religiously diverse faculty? Whither Notre Dame in, say, 2028 should it not endeavor to move in the direction suggested here, or frame a viable alternative strategy for sustaining its historic mission and identity? Only the future will answer the two foundational questions and their corollaries. The one certainty is that *it is myopic to see the secularism that has prevailed in the academy for about one century as what must be forever*. Thus the University finds itself presented it *with a rare academic opportunity. . . .*

A Catholic research university needs to create an alternative to the "Harvard-Berkeley model of excellence." . . . When people and institutions *really know themselves* and are at their best, they can feel more comfortable with people and institutions different from themselves. And sometimes they can be more generously welcoming of the other and thus grow and change themselves. The ethos that supports Notre Dame's human education has that capacity. . . . Insofar as Notre Dame's *Catholicism is learned and self-confident, it will be strong enough to support religious inclusion without demanding religious dilution, or even religion, of those who belong here.* To know oneself through and apart from the other; to *seek agreement while respecting difference*; to live together in comity *without seeking uniformity*—these phrases may sound bland and clichéd, but they evoke something of authentic cosmopolitanism, a rhetorical commonplace which is rare in life.

2

The Apparent Assumptions Behind and Implications of Notre Dame's Catholic Mission for Its Faculty

An Interpretive Commentary in Ten Proposals

IN THE PREVIOUS CHAPTER, I argued for the crucial importance of explicit, confident, and compelling visions at successful Catholic colleges and universities. I also reviewed a number of statements and documents from the University of Notre Dame that illustrate the kind of clear, strong, and consistent messages about vision that Catholic colleges and universities need to develop, express, and champion with all of their constituencies. I noted, however, that lofty visions such as those expressed at Notre Dame need to be explained in more specific statements. What do statements of vision and mission mean on an everyday basis for practice and decision-making—especially when it comes to the faculty? In this chapter, I begin to spell out answers to such questions. I will offer what seems to me to be the most obvious assumptions and implications of the Notre Dame statements examined in the previous chapter. What do they presuppose? What, more practically, do they mean for the ongoing life of Notre Dame, particularly for faculty? And how might all of this be generalized for and adapted to the particular situations of other Catholic colleges and universities?

What follows represents my own interpretation, not the official view of Notre Dame. It also aims to speak about the role of faculty, not about undergraduate or graduate students, at Notre Dame and potentially elsewhere. It is of course fallible and no doubt incomplete and inadequate, and so is open to debate and revision. That said, Notre Dame's defining statements and documents about mission and faculty, noted in the previous chapter, seem to me inescapably to entail a set of assumptions and implications that I think are worth summarizing as the basis for focused consideration and discussion. Given what those statements and documents explicitly say, it seems to follow that all (actual and prospective) members of the Notre Dame faculty ought to understand and be prepared to accept the following points:

1. *Notre Dame is in its mission attempting something genuinely unique and unusual, which sets it apart from nearly every other institution of higher education in the world.*

   Notre Dame has chosen to pursue a special and difficult mission. No seriously Catholic university has in recent history achieved or sustained preeminence as a research university in the broader field of (mostly secularized) higher education. Strong, almost irresistible sociological forces cause most religious colleges and universities to either (a) secularize on matters of faith (and prioritize research achievements—not that that necessarily leads to impressive results, as often it leads to mediocrity) *or* (b) become religiously sectarian (and sacrifice research achievements). Notre Dame can look to no successful existing models for realizing its combined goals in research, undergraduate excellence, and Catholic character.

Nevertheless, Notre Dame is committed against the odds to *both* strengthening its Catholic mission *and* achieving preeminence as a research university, as well as maintaining true excellence in undergraduate education. This unique ambition makes Notre Dame a highly distinctive context in which to serve as faculty member: it entails not only unique opportunities but also special challenges and responsibilities that simply do not exist in most other universities.

2. *Notre Dame is determined not to become secularized.*

Many Catholic institutions of higher education in the United States and abroad have become quite secular, following the common academic path of marginalizing their historic faith identities and commitments. Notre Dame is determined to resist this trend for the long run. It is committed to not become another historically Catholic college or university known for having declined significantly in the importance of its Catholic identity and commitments.

Moreover, Notre Dame is not neutral with regard to faith traditions. It will not become Catholic merely in paying lip service to a religious "heritage" or by affirming select and vague Catholic "values" (e.g., "social justice" or "honesty") that resonate with many non-Catholics as well. Notre Dame is and will remain committed to a particular Church and faith tradition, even as it builds its capacities as a research university.

Notre Dame is in this sense a *unique* institution in the field of Catholic higher education and intends to remain so.

3. *Notre Dame has every right as a private Catholic university to commit itself fully and without apology to its stated mission, to work to strengthen its Catholic character, and to intentionally build a faculty that understands and promotes its unique mission.*

If Notre Dame hopes to succeed, it of course has to pursue its goals with much realism and discernment, operating pragmatically in the mostly secularized field of higher education. Its religious vision must confront and negotiate truly challenging realities. However, as a matter of principle, Notre Dame is in fact free to pursue its mission according to its Catholic history, character, and goals (within the constraints of legitimate law and moral conduct), as long as it is prepared to accept the consequences of its institutional commitments.

More than 5,500 other institutions of higher education exist in the United States, most of which are not Catholic. Notre Dame bears no obligation to become like them. While the university may choose (precisely for reasons stated in its mission) to encourage and accommodate a great deal of legitimate diversity among its faculty, it is under no obligation to faculty who do not support its goals to concede or adjust its Catholic mission on their behalf. Notre Dame may have to pay some consequences for acting on this fact, but that itself does not justify Notre Dame's diverting from its stated mission.

4. *Very many US academics outside of Notre Dame will not understand, appreciate, or value Notre Dame's mission; indeed, many are suspicious, if not antagonistic,*

*toward it. That does matter, but it cannot become the
most important fact influencing Notre Dame's activities
and goals.*

In the broadly secularized climate of higher education in the West today, there is no way that Notre
Dame can pursue its Catholic mission without some
hostility, resistance, and opposition from people who
cannot understand or abide it. Liberal political theory
and culture have largely succeeded in the West in
defining "religion" as an exclusively private matter of
personal opinion that bears no epistemic authority,
contributes nothing to the knowledge of humankind,
and cannot justly influence policy of any public or (in
some people's minds) even private institutional importance. Catholicism claims a very different view on
the matter, however, as Notre Dame's mission documents make clear. They assume and declare, for example, that faith and reason are not only compatible
but are both required to achieve movement toward
the fullness of truth, that the Catholic Church bears
a millennia-old intellectual tradition (from which
Western universities historically originated) that
speaks to most areas of university learning, and that
the Christian faith entails moral imperatives relevant
in both private and public life.

Given these extensive disagreements, many
people today, especially those in US higher education, will not (at least in the short run) understand,
entertain, or value Notre Dame's Catholic mission.
And that will sometimes make life for faculty at Notre
Dame uncomfortable and difficult. This anti-Catholic
bias will likely also (unjustly) hurt the university on
some measures of research excellence. Notre Dame
intends as much as possible to establish open, friendly,

constructive relations with scholars and institutions in the field of US higher education and beyond. Any alienation or antagonism will not originate from Notre Dame. At the same time, the university cannot compromise its Catholic character and mission simply in order to be liked, accepted by, or seemingly relevant to the broader academic world. Notre Dame needs to develop on its own terms, not those given by outside cultures and traditions. The field of higher education in the United States does not need yet one more conformist university, so Notre Dame should confidently participate in higher education oriented by its own imperatives and sensibilities. In that way it will have the greatest chance of making a distinctive contribution over time to higher education and the broader world.

An informed acceptance of these facts and a readiness to work with them, even when it is difficult, are necessary in all areas of faculty concern, from new faculty recruitment, to status building in disciplines, to developing systems of rewarding valuable faculty contributions. As noted below, the standards for some, if not many, faculty at Notre Dame will therefore be even higher than at most mainstream universities because of the distinctive and sometimes countercultural nature of Notre Dame's unique Catholic mission.

5. *Notre Dame faculty may legitimately support the university's mission in one of two valuable ways, either (1) (for those most committed) by actively endorsing and contributing toward its realization, or (2) (for those less invested) by tacitly supporting the mission by using their particular valuable gifts (i.e., teaching, researching, service, etc.) and not actively impeding the mission.*

Notre Dame's documents about mission and faculty state clearly that the university welcomes a vast diversity of positions and perspectives in its faculty. That attitude, it affirms, is necessary in order to be truly "catholic," to provide top-notch undergraduate education, and to become a premier research university. Notre Dame has no interest in being sectarian, parochial, exclusivist, or intellectually cloistered. Among other things, this means that not all faculty members have to be "true believers" in and proactive supporters of the Catholic dimension of Notre Dame's mission. Notre Dame can well achieve its mission with—and indeed will positively benefit from having—some (though not a preponderance of) doubters and skeptics on its faculty. Such faculty members are not and should not be considered second-class citizens on campus.

However, Notre Dame faculty who have not "bought into" the mission nevertheless bear the responsibility to acknowledge the mission and avoid actively resisting or undermining it. It is possible and worthwhile for scholars to contribute to Notre Dame's mission by teaching, researching, publishing, being good colleagues, and serving Notre Dame in various other ways—without being leading proponents of the mission. Those faculty who are not personally committed to Notre Dame's Catholic mission can tacitly cooperate with the pursuit and realization of the mission by others who are more committed to it. But it would positively violate Notre Dame's mission, and therefore be a breach of the good faith contract implied in one's faculty status, to intentionally obstruct or undermine that mission.

6. *Serving as a faculty member at Notre Dame is not an*

entitlement or an obligation but rather an opportunity to be voluntarily embraced and recurrently affirmed with an awareness of the implications of Notre Dame's Catholic character and mission.

There is no reason why Notre Dame faculty members should be in the dark about the fact that Notre Dame is a seriously Catholic university, or unaware that this fact has institutional and cultural consequences. Notre Dame has made its Catholic history, character, and mission publicly known in multiple ways for a long time. Notre Dame only does itself and others a disservice if it hedges or refuses to speak clearly about its Catholic character, commitments, and mission. All new faculty are entitled to a full explanation of what they are getting into; and they, for their part, are responsible to seriously discern whether Notre Dame is the right place of work for them. If current or prospective Notre Dame faculty members decide that they cannot even tacitly support the university's mission, they are of course free to leave or to decline a job offer (if an offer is made despite their opposition to the mission).

Again, there are more than 5,500 other institutions of higher education in the United States today that do not share Notre Dame's particular vision, among which faculty who decide they do not belong at Notre Dame might seek employment. In that context, the choice to serve as faculty at Notre Dame implies, by way of an informal but real social contract, a readiness to constructively come to terms with Notre Dame's Catholic character and purposes (as well as the other features of its mission). Faculty who want the benefits of working at Notre Dame but who actively oppose, disparage, and undermine its mission are living in bad faith in relation to the university, its students, and their more committed colleagues.

Similarly, scholars who came to Notre Dame in previous eras, when its Catholic character may not have been as strong as it is today and will become in the future, simply have to accept that all institutions evolve one way or another over time, that nobody in any employment sector is guaranteed to work for an institution that will never change, and that the burden is on them to reckon with the consequences of Notre Dame's evolving (and strengthening) Catholic character and mission. Furthermore, ex-Catholics and dissenting Catholics on the faculty at Notre Dame who may be embittered or antagonistic toward the Catholic Church need to exercise particular self-reflexivity and prudent restraint in order to contribute to Notre Dame's mission in constructive (even if also critical) ways. To benefit from a faculty position even while using it to attack and tear down the university or the Church it serves is a duplicitous act that cannot be good for anyone involved.

7. *Not every scholar or teacher in the country can or should serve as a faculty member at Notre Dame.*

As much as the culture of liberal individualism abhors the idea of "discrimination," it remains true nonetheless that Notre Dame is not for everyone and that not everyone belongs at Notre Dame. Some forms of discrimination are bad and immoral, while others, under discrimination's more neutral definition (i.e., making intelligent judgments about meaningful differences), are useful and legitimate. The key is to be thoughtful about which is operative when.

With this in mind, it must be acknowledged that not everyone is qualified or well-fitted for Notre

Dame, for a variety of reasons. And Notre Dame is not a good fit for every imaginable scholar or teacher. That is fine. Likewise, not everyone belongs on the faculty of every public secular, Jewish, Muslim, Mormon, or evangelical college or university either. When structural pluralism is justly practiced, it is healthy for American higher education and society.

That Notre Dame is not a good fit for some faculty and vice-versa does not mean, however, that Notre Dame or the faculty member is somehow lesser in value or worthiness. Rather, a poor fit is often a matter of divergent goals, priorities, and needs. Among the various criteria that prospective faculty and Notre Dame should use to evaluate their fit is the extent to which the prospective faculty can support Notre Dame's mission, including its core Catholic dimension and implications. Faculty jobs should be offered to and accepted by scholars who understand and can in good faith contribute constructively to the mission, whether actively or tacitly. Deans and department chairs have a particular responsibility in recruitment to ensure that they and prospective faculty understand and take into account this factor.

Furthermore, as noted above, by virtue of its uniquely ambitious mission, Notre Dame demands much more of faculty than most other US colleges and universities. To succeed at most good public and private research universities, faculty must be very good scholars and adequate teachers. To succeed at good liberal arts colleges, faculty must be very good scholars and very good teachers. To succeed at many second- and third-tier colleges and universities, faculty must be adequate teachers and scholars. At Notre Dame, successful faculty who desire to further the university's Catholic mission must be very good scholars, very good teachers, *and* capable of contributing to the religious dimension of Notre Dame's mission. The standard is in this way set higher for some, if not many, Notre Dame faculty, especially those who aid in forming the academic life and culture of Notre Dame.

8. *Diversity among the Notre Dame faculty exists not for its own sake, much less as a way to dilute or "tone down" the Catholic character of the university, but rather as a means of making the university "catholic" (small c)—that is, home to a broad range of perspectives, voices, and insights stemming from a variety of social, cultural, (non)religious, racial, ethnic, and gender statuses, which collectively help Notre Dame move toward a fuller understanding of truth.*

Notre Dame has repeatedly expressed its desire to build a faculty diverse in outlook as well as in racial, ethnic, gender, and social background. That is not, however, because Notre Dame is beholden to the demands of secular multiculturalism or any other ideology or interest group. It is rather because the right kind of diversity strengthens and actually constitutes in part Notre Dame's own Catholic educational, social, and ecclesial mission. "Catholic" means "universal," and the Catholic Church does not exclude from its community any person who is seeking or open to seeking the truth. And seeking the truth is best accomplished through the exchange and engagement, both cooperative and sometimes conflictive, of different points of view (ideally within a shared framework of assumptions, evidence, and reason). Faculty diversity at Notre Dame thus ought to be understood as normatively grounded in and governed by the particular logic of the Catholic tradition, not as autonomously self-authenticated or demanded by some external ideology.

9. *To actively support Notre Dame's mission, faculty must have, among other things, a familiarity with Catholicism and a willingness to engage in ongoing discussion about the relationship of Christian faith and human reason in theology, science, and other fields.*

The Notre Dame mission requires its community members to engage in informed dialogue toward the pursuit of truth. Since it is a Catholic institution, that exchange sometimes centers on the active engagement of faith and reason, which requires participants to be knowledgeable about the Christian faith. A lack of familiarity with the religious issues at hand will result in participants merely sharing their ignorance or talking past each other. Not all faculty, but a preponderance of Notre Dame faculty—including a significant portion of faculty distributed in each college and department—ought to spend time learning from and about basic informative texts (including the Notre Dame documents noted above, the Catechism of the Catholic Church, Catholic social teachings, etc.).

Non-Catholic faculty, whether religious or not, who wish to take an *active* role in the life of the Notre Dame academic community should be prepared to engage Catholicism, to challenge Catholicism when appropriate from their perspective, and to have their own perspectives challenged by Catholic truth claims and arguments. Faculty who choose not to familiarize themselves with Catholic teachings in matters of relevance to their academic work thus voluntarily remove themselves from being able to offer qualified, informed arguments in the dialogues, discussions, and arguments under consideration.

In short, engaging some of the key issues that Notre Dame has defined as truly mattering requires (at least) a basic education in the substance of the issues—including theological issues—in question. Faculty in various disciplines are called to explore the particular dimensions of the interface of faith, knowledge, and reason that pertain to their areas of expertise. For this reason, Notre Dame faculty have extra cause to pursue ongoing inter-disciplinary learning, insofar as broad familiarity with theology, philosophy, history, ethics, law, social theory, and so on helps advance the university's mission. By contrast, hyper-specialization will inhibit the kinds of discussions required by that mission.

10. *When Notre Dame is apparently not living up to its own calling and potential as a Catholic institution, attempts by faculty to reform the university are important, valuable, and necessary; however, normally they ought to appeal to the beliefs, standards, and morals of ("within") the Catholic tradition (against what may be Notre Dame's failing or substandard practices) rather than to alien, "external" assumptions, commitments, and standards.*

Like all human institutions, Notre Dame must continually be held accountable for its practices and, when necessary, critiqued and reformed so that it can better reach its goals and fulfill its potential. But institutional reform should aim at helping the university more faithfully realize its constitutive mission, not at making it a fundamentally different institution. The latter kind of change amounts to a "hostile takeover" that disrespects Notre Dame's institutional right to self-definition and determination. Notre Dame must of course always be open to reasoned critique from within and without. But the standards of critique used as leverage by faculty seeking institutional change ought—on both pragmatic and principled grounds—to be standards "internal" to Notre Dame's Catholic identity and commitments, not "external" to it.

The matters addressed here can be difficult to discuss and pursue, especially for faculty who conceive of themselves as autonomous intellectuals, rather than as belonging to a community of scholars who stand accountable to the institutions that employ them and provide them with students. But Catholic colleges and universities must engage these difficult matters, or else relations on campus come to resemble a dysfunctional family in which certain people cannot talk to other people about a whole list of sensitive issues.

I understand that there are faculty and administrators at Catholic colleges and universities who may oppose my suggestions. Perhaps they (1) object to their school's prioritizing its Catholic mission, (2) want their school to tone down its Catholic character to become more like secular universities, (3) feel uncomfortable with the potential consequences of their school's Catholic commitments for their careers, (4) believe they are entitled to work at their schools even if they ignore, undermine, or oppose the official Catholic mission, (5) feel that their schools should conform to the demands of secular liberal multiculturalism or similar ideologies even when doing so would violate basic Catholic teachings, or (6) see their schools as a target and vehicle for political activism aimed to undermine its Catholic character, mission, and moral commitments. Such faculty and administrators, I think, need to face their situations more realistically and accept the consequences. This chapter is offered in an effort to promote the reflections and discussions that effort entails, however difficult the matters and implications may be.

3

How Faculty Can Support the Catholic Mission

(Even If They Are Not Catholic or Do Not Understand or Personally Endorse the Catholic Mission)

INTRODUCTION

How can Notre Dame faculty support the University in its Catholic mission? (And how might faculty at other Catholic colleges and universities support their schools in their missions?) That is surely an easier question to answer for faculty who are practicing Catholics and who understand and believe in Notre Dame's Catholic mission. But what about those who practice other religious faiths or no faith? What of faculty who are not familiar with the idea of a university rooted in a particular church tradition? And what about faculty who do not understand the Catholic part of Notre Dame's mission, or understand it but cannot personally endorse it?

I attempt here to provide some constructive answers to those questions, in hopes of minimizing possible misunderstanding among prospective and current faculty, widening the embrace of Notre Dame's vision by its faculty, and helping to advance the achievement of Notre Dame's mission in all its aspects.

As I noted above, the University of Notre Dame has committed itself to a particular three-part goal, in the words of President John Jenkins, of "becoming a preeminent research university with a distinctive Catholic mission and an unsurpassed undergraduate education." Unique among the country's universities, Notre Dame ambitiously seeks not only to become a great research university while sustaining its quality of undergraduate education—a challenge difficult enough for most schools—but also to strengthen its Catholic character and intellectual life. Notre Dame's mission, according to its statement of "Vision and Goals," involves the responsibility to "ensure that the University's Catholic character informs all its endeavors." That is a tall order. Yet the president, the provost, the board of trustees, and other leaders of Notre Dame are committed to achieving the university's stated mission, including its Catholic component. And they have asked *all* Notre Dame faculty to support that mission in good faith, in a variety of ways.

The members of the faculty at Notre Dame hopefully know what it means to help Notre Dame maintain excellence in undergraduate education and become a preeminent research university. The challenges of those two aspects of the mission are standard and widely understood in US higher education. But what about the third part of Notre Dame's mission: strengthening its Catholic character and ensuring that all it does is informed by the Catholic tradition? Can *all* faculty support that?

The answer that a host of Notre Dame statements and documents on the matter have given is, "Yes, all faculty can support Notre Dame's Catholic mission." In his 2006 address to the faculty, for example, President Jenkins insisted that "every member of our faculty, Catholic or not, can contribute to the religious mission of this University." In fact, Notre Dame's position is that all of its faculty not only can but also *must* support the Catholic mission, one way or another. I agree with that. But declaring that so does not make clear how faculty—particularly non-Catholic faculty and those who do not understand or harbor serious reservations about Notre Dame's Catholic mission—can practically support it in good faith. My purpose here is to spell out how that is possible, what it might look like, and what normative guidance it gives to Notre Dame faculty members as they conduct their work in service to the university.

As preliminary background, it will be useful to remind ourselves of some basic facts that bear on the matter by briefly recapping the ideas of the previous chapter. First, Notre Dame is attempting something unique, which sets it apart from nearly every other institution of higher education in the world. Second, Notre Dame is determined to avoid becoming another historically Catholic university known for assigning declining significance to its Catholic identity. Third, as a private Catholic university, Notre Dame has every right to commit itself without apology to its stated mission, to work to strengthen its Catholic character, and to build a faculty that understands and promotes its mission. Fourth, many academics outside of Notre Dame will never understand, appreciate, or value Notre Dame's mission; some will be suspicious of, if not antagonistic, toward it—a reality that does matter, but that cannot become the most important fact influencing Notre Dame's mission. Fifth, serving as a faculty member at Notre Dame is not an entitlement or obligation but rather an opportunity one may voluntarily embrace with an awareness of the nature of Notre Dame's mission. And, sixth, not every scholar or teacher in the country can or should serve as a faculty member at Notre Dame: Our Lady's university is exactly right for some people, adequately right for others, but really not right for others, and that is okay.

These may be either obvious or difficult things to say and hear, depending on the reader's position, but in any case they are basic facts about Notre Dame that faculty should understand if they hope to know what Notre Dame is and where it is going. With that background in mind, I return to the central question. First, I give the easier answers. How can practicing Catholic faculty and those who understand and personally embrace Notre Dame's Catholic mission actively support it? The answers to that question are myriad, many of which are suggested in Notre Dame's official statements and documents on the matter.

HOW FACULTY WHO UNDERSTAND AND EMBRACE THE CATHOLIC MISSION CAN SUPPORT IT

Notre Dame faculty who understand and embrace the Catholic mission, perhaps especially if they are committed Catholics themselves, can support it in many ways. They can learn more theology, understanding its central integrative function at a Catholic university. They can think long and hard about how their particular areas of expertise bear on Catholic teaching and practice. In this, they can actively engage in the ongoing "dialogue of faith and reason" when it comes to their professional and scholarly expertise, exploring what some call the "integration of faith and learning." Such faculty can help Notre Dame be a place "where the Church does its thinking," where truth is pursued within a Catholic (and, more broadly, Christian) framework of understanding. More generally, faculty, especially Catholics, who understand and embrace Notre Dame's Catholic mission can work to develop intellectually coherent ways of thinking about the unity of truth and the ultimate coherence of all knowledge.

Notre Dame faculty actively committed to Notre Dame's Catholic mission can form disciplinary and inter-disciplinary workshops as well as study and discussion groups of faculty and students to explore in depth some aspect of the Catholic Church tradition as it relates to their intellectual interests. Such faculty can proactively foster inter-faith and religious–secular dialogue with colleagues on campus in order to promote deeper mutual understanding across different boundaries of religious faith and unbelief. They can choose to engage in scholarship and teaching that directly serves the well-being of the Catholic Church. And they can devote their time and energy to helping to recruit other faculty committed to the mission.

Notre Dame faculty who believe in the Catholic mission, especially committed Catholic faculty, can also model (presumably) mature lives of faith for their students expressed in their relationships, worship, scholarly endeavors, service, and beyond. Such faculty can devote time and effort to deepening their theological understandings of Catholic teachings, both to mature in faith personally and to share with students. They can support and be involved in various campus and off-campus Catholic pastoral and social service ministries. They can talk with students about issues of faith and doubt, as they are able and as is appropriate. They can join with other Notre Dame participants in the annual

March for Life and other national events of representation and dialogue. They can open their classes with brief prayers. And they can participate actively in the Catholic liturgical life of the Notre Dame community on campus and nearby.

In these and a variety of other ways, faculty at Notre Dame who understand and personally embrace the Catholic mission of the university can actively support that mission by their presence and in their work. To succeed in its mission, Notre Dame needs a "preponderance" of such faculty.

At the same time, however, a significant proportion of Notre Dame's faculty need *not* take this approach, but can support the Catholic mission in other ways.

HOW FACULTY WHO DO NOT UNDERSTAND OR ENDORSE THE CATHOLIC MISSION CAN SUPPORT IT NEVERTHELESS

Notre Dame's leaders have indicated in many places how faculty who don't comprehend or don't believe in Notre Dame's Catholic mission can, as first-class, fully valued members of the faculty, nonetheless help advance that mission in good faith. Such faculty can support the mission *tacitly* rather than actively in a wide variety of ways. But some general principles, with both positive and negative aspects, will no doubt apply.

On the *positive* side, tacitly supporting Notre Dame's Catholic mission means:

1. working to understand the Catholic mission as well as reasonably possible (such as by studying the relevant Notre Dame statements and documents on the matter),

2. accepting that the Catholic mission is an integral part

of the university, even if not all faculty are actively invested in it,

3. allowing colleagues who *do* understand and believe in the mission to work to advance it,

4. understanding that Notre Dame has a constitutive, two-way relationship with the Catholic Church,

5. supporting the need to prioritize the hiring of excellent Catholic faculty (along with women and racial and ethnic minorities),

6. exercising faculty voting rights on issues related to the Catholic mission, especially on hiring, *as if* one did generally believe in the Catholic mission,

7. providing models to newer faculty for ways the Catholic mission may be supported even by those who do not personally embrace it, and

8. finding as many ways as possible to actively support the other two aspects of Notre Dame's larger (three-part) mission.

In this way, some Notre Dame faculty members might say, "I do not really understand this Catholic-mission business and/or I don't think I believe in it or that I am prepared to advance it. Nevertheless, I will do my best as a researching and publishing scholar, as a teacher of undergraduate and graduate students, and as a good citizen of the university to help Notre Dame advance as a 'preeminent research university' offering 'unsurpassed undergraduate education.' Meanwhile, I'll let those invested in the Catholic mission do their thing."

Such a general approach to supporting Notre Dame's mission is, as the university has made clear, *absolutely legitimate, indispensable, appreciated, and prized at Notre Dame.* Faculty who take this approach to advancing Notre

Dame's larger mission are *first-class* citizens just like those who actively support the Catholic mission. Furthermore, it must be said that there is not only one way to support the Catholic mission more passively. Different faculty can tacitly support the mission in a variety of ways, as long as the general contours and vision of that approach are clear.

Tacitly supporting Notre Dame's Catholic mission also entails a *negative* aspect. On this negative side, tacit support means:

1. not disparaging or obstructing efforts by others at Notre Dame to realize the Catholic mission,

2. not covertly or openly undermining, resisting, or attacking the Catholic mission,

3. not recklessly disparaging the Catholic Church and its holistic mission in the world,

4. not supporting efforts to secularize Notre Dame or undermine its Catholic institutional character,

5. not believing that truth does not exist and so cannot be intelligently pursued in an academic context,

6. not offering criticisms of Notre Dame that are essentially destructive of its Catholic theological orientation and culture (instead offering constructive criticisms, which are of course necessary and important, and framing criticism in terms of Notre Dame's own standards and goods, not some alien tradition).

In short, tacit support for Notre Dame's Catholic mission in its negative dimension requires allowing others to actively pursue and advance the mission, even though one cannot personally contribute to that effort, and avoiding working against their efforts. Notre Dame faculty members might thus say, "I am not personally 'bought into' Notre Dame's Catholic mission, but in recognition of the Catholic character and mission of the university that employs me, I will not act in ways that obstruct, undermine, or denigrate that mission. Rather, I will focus on contributing to the university in other important ways." Again, faculty take this stance are very much needed, welcomed, and respected at Notre Dame. They are as entitled to first-class faculty status as anyone else, and perhaps deserve extra recognition for voluntarily acting with integrity and intelligence in such an unusual academic situation.

WHAT SUPPORT FOR THE CATHOLIC MISSION RULES OUT

Both my discussion, and the official Notre Dame statements that I reviewed in chapter 2, make clear that a necessary (though not sufficient) condition of employment as a member of the faculty at Notre Dame is a willingness to support the university's Catholic mission. That support may be active or it may be tacit, as described above; both options are fully legitimate and valuable and can be expressed in a variety of ways. However, by contrast, support for Notre Dame's Catholic mission may *not* be simply non-existent. Ruled out of bounds by Notre Dame's mission is absolute indifference or definite hostility to its Catholic mission on the part of faculty.

At Notre Dame, unlike nearly every other university in the world, when it comes to an orientation toward Catholicism in higher education, not everything goes. Notre Dame, in seeking to be authentically "catholic" (i.e., universal) and Catholic, is highly inclusive in many ways. But the university's mission makes certain demands, a fact that current and prospective faculty must accept.

Prospective faculty who do not support Notre Dame's Catholic mission should not be offered faculty positions;

and they, on the basis of conscience, should not accept a job at Notre Dame (if they are offered one) unless they are ready to seriously reconsider their view and come to at least tacitly support that Catholic mission, in ways described above.

The more difficult case involves *current* faculty who definitely are not willing or able to support the Catholic mission. In some circumstances, such faculty should consider seeking employment at a university that is more suited to their beliefs and commitments, which would be better for all involved. Other circumstances, though, may be more complicated. In any case, however, the larger principle stands that all faculty at Notre Dame are asked to support all three dimensions of Notre Dame's mission, including the crucial Catholic aspect. At the very least, tacit support is necessary; no faculty member is entitled willfully to directly or indirectly obstruct that mission.

CONCLUSION

It is entirely possible and fully worthwhile for faculty members at Notre Dame to contribute to Notre Dame's mission without being proponents of its Catholic dimension, simply by teaching, researching, and publishing well, being good faculty colleagues, and serving Notre Dame in various other ways. Notre Dame does need a significant proportion of its faculty to understand, invest in, and work to advance its Catholic mission. But no given faculty member has to do that. And those who do not, yet who make valuable contributions to Notre Dame's larger mission in other ways, deserve to be honored as first-class, indispensable citizens in the Notre Dame community. Complete indifference or opposition to Notre Dame's Catholic mission, on the other hand, does not fit what the university is and where it is going. All faculty have the responsibility to understand and prudently choose how best to respond to these matters.

4

Social Science in Catholic Higher Education

What Difference Does Catholicism Make?

GIVEN THE SECULAR OUTLOOK that has taken over Western higher education in the last hundred years, many faculty and administrators, even at Catholic universities and colleges, cannot imagine what it might mean to take a distinctively *Catholic* approach to the social sciences, among other fields of scholarship. For many, all that "being a Catholic university" could possibly entail is hosting various Catholic campus ministries, Masses, guest speakers and forums, and architectural styles and artistic objects on campus. This we might call the "*extracurricular*" conception of Catholic higher education. Others may assume that universities and colleges are Catholic insofar as they represent and teach certain "values," such as honesty, compassion, peace, and justice. This we might call the "*Catholic values*" approach. Yet others understand certain universities and colleges to be Catholic because their general education curricula include a required core theology course or two. This we might consider the "*theology requirement*" view of Catholic higher education.

All three of these views reflect important parts of a Catholic higher education. Catholic universities and colleges should have Catholic extracurricular activities and artifacts, represent and teach Catholic values, and require that students learn theology. But that does not exhaust what it means to be a Catholic university or college—it does not even get close to the heart of the matter. For the heart of any university or college's life is not extracurricular programming or an emphasis on certain "values" but intellectual inquiry, scholarship, and teaching. So where Catholicism as a distinctive approach to life and the world does not significantly influence those centers of academic life, then those universities and colleges cannot meaningfully call themselves "Catholic." For a university or college to be recognizably *Catholic*, the Catholic tradition has to form its intellectual inquiry, academic scholarship, and classroom teaching.

But doesn't this represent the illegitimate intrusion of faith into science, the mixing of subjective belief and personal opinions with actual knowledge of facts? No. In fact, we have very good reasons for sustaining creative, reasoned, mutual engagement of the Catholic Church's tradition and the contemporary social sciences. What are they?

First, Roman Catholicism actually *invented* the university as an institution in the Latin West—in Paris, Oxford, Bologna, Salamanca, and Cambridge, among other places. The Catholic Church, far from being a misplaced tag-along in universities, actually conceived of and founded all of the first universities of Europe, which flourished for the better part of a millennium before being taken over by secular interests. The more distant roots of the modern university go as far back as the sixth century, with the formation of Christian cathedral and monastic schools across Europe, which developed during the medieval era as the predecessors of the later emergent universities. This was no accident. The logic of the Catholic faith stimulated and encouraged rigorous intellectual inquiry, even as it does now. That some universities today wish to be distinctively Catholic in their intellectual life is, therefore, no oddity, but the long-term norm of higher education in the West.

Second, excellent arguments exist for the full compatibility, even concord, of Christian truth claims with the best practices and knowledge of modern science. The Scientific Revolution in the West was advanced primarily by Christian intellectuals who assumed that the universe had an order and intelligibility by virtue of being God's creation. With few exceptions, modern science developed in the West having minimal conflict with religion, even after Darwin. It was not until the *late* nineteenth century, when a generation of anti-religious scientific activists (along with some help from cooperative religious voices) began pushing hard their atheism, naturalism, materialism, and positivism—which are philosophical, even metaphysical, not properly scientific, beliefs—that conflicts between science and religion became really pronounced. The "inevitable warfare of science and religion" myth that so many moderns have come to believe is in fact a fiction, the fabricated narrative of late-nineteenth century anti-religious activists in science who were struggling to gain power over the religious perspectives they were seeking to marginalize.

Third, science is in fact inherently incapable of judging the validity of most of Christianity's core theological truth claims, since even trying to do that requires stepping outside of the proper competence of science and entering the quite different realms of metaphysics and theology. To say that God does or does not exist is not a scientific claim but a metaphysical or theological one. Scientists are of course entitled to believe and make metaphysical and theological truth claims, but they should not confuse those with scientific claims. To think that *science* can demonstrate Christianity (or even theism) to be false reflects a massive slippage in basic reasoning—ironically, often in the name of "reason."

Fourth, Catholicism is not merely the private religious "faith" of certain individuals today—as it is frequently viewed by those outside it—but a deep, rich, and complex tradition of philosophical, historical, social, political, psychological, economic, legal, architectural, and aesthetic reflection, creativity, and engagement. Notwithstanding the fact that, like every long-lived human institution, the Catholic Church has engaged in its share of blunders and errors, the Catholic faith still possesses immense intellectual resources to bring to bear on making sense of the human condition past, present, and future. There is no good reason why that tradition cannot legitimately engage the intellectual work at the heart of the contemporary university or college.

Fifth, we must recognize that modern social science operates on the basis of certain philosophical assumptions that science itself cannot verify. Behind every social science program stands some presupposed, knowledge-governing belief commitments that are ultimately based on something like faith. Most social scientists know that all theories are "value-laden," that there exists no "view from nowhere" from which to conduct neutral and objective social science, and that scientific research is always governed by larger "paradigms" that define the relevant interests, questions, evidence, interpretations, and explanations.

Less commonly acknowledged, however, is the fact that modern philosophy's goal of identifying a foundation for human knowledge that is indubitably certain and universally binding on all rational persons (commonly known as "foundationalism") has failed—and that, because no such foundation for certain knowledge exists, social scientists must work as well as they can to sort out with an open mind the validity and fruitfulness of multiple, rival presupposed approaches undergirding the advancement of knowledge. This means, among other things, that the old assumption in higher education that secular truth claims are automatically more valid than religious ones is simply untenable. The previous epistemic privileging of secularism no longer enjoys a defensible basis, so the belief systems undergirding valid human knowledge-seeking must include alternative approaches, including the Catholic tradition. (That is, unless universities are interested in censorship to defend a parochial world of narrow, exclusively secular ideas.)

Sixth, even Catholic social science faculty who dissent from the Church on certain issues or who wish to protect strong academic freedoms at Catholic colleges and universities need not generalize those concerns into sweeping opposition or hostility to the Church and its tradition, especially in ways that ignore the vast possibilities for thinking as *Catholic* scholars about their academic disciplines.[15] The liberal Catholic writer, Peter Steinfels, said it well: "Liberal Catholicism has failed to match its understandable concern for preserving academic freedom in Catholic colleges and universities with any comparable passion about preserving the distinctive mission and character of these institutions as

15. A smart, creative, and historically well-informed reconsideration of the meaning of academic freedom in Catholic higher education is Kenneth Garcia, *Academic Freedom and the Telos of the Catholic University* (New York: Palgrave MacMillan, 2012).

places where Catholic thought, art, literature, perspectives on society, and reflections on science could be freely pursued at the depth unlikely to occur in secular institutions."[16] One can be a liberal Catholic and also be deeply committed to the strong Catholic mission of one's university or college when it comes to the intellectual work of being a scholar and teacher. Holding critical views of some Catholic Church teachings need not translate into generalized opposition to the distinctively Catholic mission of one's college or university.

I propose that social scientists at Catholic universities and colleges today should take seriously and work out the implications of these six observations. What then, more specifically, might it mean for the Catholic tradition to shape a university or college's intellectual inquiry, academic scholarship, and classroom teaching in social science and beyond? Among the many possibilities are the following:

Commitment to Truth in Realism: The conduct of social science at a Catholic university or college must proceed on the belief that the end goal of all human inquiry is *to understand what is true about what is real as best as is humanly possible*. This means, at a minimum, rejecting epistemological skepticism, deconstructionism, relativism, nihilism, and apathy. It means not being afraid to talk about truth, even while being appropriately cautious in speaking about Truth. It also means not resting content with the apparent incoherence of perspectives and knowledge across academic disciplines and fields, but instead seeking intellectual coherence and integration where possible. The Catholic university or college is engaged in a search for the truth about reality in all of its complexity; all involved in the university must see this as the proper end of the university's

16. Peter Steinfels, "Reinventing Liberal Catholicism," *Commonweal*, November 19, 1999, 38.

activities. Such an approach is not unique to—but certainly must characterize—Catholic universities and colleges.

Self-Reflexive Epistemological Humility: Social scientists in a Catholic university or college need to maintain a constant awareness of the limits, partial character, and fallibility of all social scientific knowledge. This task involves, among other things, rejecting the impossibility and imperialistic tendencies of scien*tistic* (an ideology of excessive trust in a particular kind of science as the only source of valid knowledge) beliefs in "objectivity," positivist certainty, and reductionistic "nothing-buttery." It also means affirming the complementarity of different forms of human insight, knowledge, and representation, including those pursued in the humanities and the arts. Such an approach is also not unique to Catholic institutions of higher education, but definitely must inform any Catholic university or college.

Interrogating Deep Disciplinary Assumptions: Conducting social science in a Catholic university or college will also require identifying and critically evaluating the inherited philosophical, normative, and (a) theological assumptions and frameworks that define and guide the disciplines. This will involve, among other things, questioning their adequacy in light of Catholic views of reality and human life, as well as seeking to revise those governing presuppositions and frameworks in light of that critical inquiry. The point is not to oppose social science, but to use the rich Catholic tradition that claims to represent truth as one means to improve social science. This work of reflexive self-criticism concerning deep assumptions in the social sciences is rarely undertaken in universities today. Few social scientists, even Catholic ones, probably even know what this means, although some models of such criticism exist. But engaging in this kind of disciplinary self-criticism is vitally necessary in a Catholic university or college and is likely to set it apart from most secular universities.

Learning Outside of Single Disciplines: Social scientists at Catholic universities and colleges need to continually learn about other academic disciplines in order to accomplish these goals. Scholars in most other universities can succeed in their careers and serve their universities (actually, *multi*versities, if not *chaos*versities), at least according to normal standards, by focusing only on the literatures of their own disciplines—thus reinforcing the hyper-specialization and über-fragmentation of knowledge in contemporary higher education. But a Catholic university or college cannot succeed in a super-specialized and fragmented state. Catholicism commends the unity and coherence of truth. Faculty thus need not only to excel in their own disciplines, but to "go the extra mile" by learning enough philosophy and theology (and probably other disciplines) to engage well in necessary higher-level critical and integrative work. Social science faculty should be especially well versed in the substance of Catholic social teachings. Catholic *uni*versity and college faculty may not need to become true "renaissance" women and men, but they do need to transcend their parochial disciplinary silos and learn enough from other fields to be able to creatively criticize and improve their own. Only extremely rarely is this done in mainstream social science today, although it is essential for the work of any Catholic university or college.

Teaching and Modeling the Intellectual Interchange between the Catholic Tradition and Academic Scholarship: Social scientists at a Catholic university or college must teach their students, especially undergraduates, about the value and means of engaging the claims of Catholicism and the social sciences in mutually constructive and critical dialogue. Students need to be disabused of the common falsehoods that the Catholic tradition has little or nothing to say about the broad range of disciplined human inquiry into truth, that science and religion are locked in an inevitable conflict of interests, and that committed Christians as a group are not as realistic about the facts of life and the world as are secularists. Mutually enriching conversations between Catholicism and social science can be—and must be in any Catholic university or college—taught and modeled in lectures, discussions, assigned readings, informal conversations, field trips, course projects, and in faculty's own published research.

Respectful Engagement with Church Teachings: When the social sciences at a Catholic university or college suggest insights or produce findings that seem to stand in tension with Catholic Church teachings, the faculty in those disciplines should exercise care and discernment in helping students (especially undergraduates) to make sense of the findings' possibilities and implications. Faculty obviously cannot minimize or suppress those difficult insights or findings in the name of protecting the Church. Everyone must be after the truth. But neither should faculty present those ideas in simple, hasty, or overconfident ways that readily undermine Church teachings or the faith of students. The Catholic Church not only teaches the unity and coherence of all truth, but understands itself as progressively learning the truth about reality in greater fullness under the hand of divine providence, in part through the unfolding of human experience in history and a growing understanding of nature. The Church has nothing to fear from genuine truths discovered by the sciences conducted rightly. At the same time, everyone must remember that reality is extremely complex; many scientific puzzles take a long time to fully understand and resolve; sometimes what seem like social scientific facts are later discredited; and oftentimes views that once seemed in tension with Christian truth claims later come to be rightly understood as compatible. Well-equipped faculty of goodwill at Catholic universities and colleges can play crucial roles in helping the Church, students, and others to sort out difficult matters with intellectual integrity in such cases. Doing so, however, requires an adequate respect for Catholic teachings, patient engagement, and wise discernment in struggling with the mutually engaging ideas and claims of the Catholic tradition and the social sciences.

Choosing Scholarly Concerns: Social scientists at Catholic universities and colleges may choose to study and teach about specific topics that are of particular interest to the Catholic Church and Christian believers. In fact, many people assume this to be the obvious (and perhaps only) way that a university or college can be "Catholic" in its intellectual work—namely, by studying things that interest Catholics. Therein lies the danger of defining only *some* matters as "Catholic topics"—and, by implication, the others as "secular"—when in fact Catholicism views all of reality as originally created good by God and worthy of serious investigation. That concern notwithstanding, it does seem appropriate that certain matters would be of special concern at a Catholic university or college, including but not limited to, for example, research on human development, the common good, family, education, morality, social and economic justice, the promotion of peace, religion and spirituality, poverty, human dignity, subsidiarity, the protection of life, and so on.

Obviously, not all social science faculty in a Catholic university or college need to or can do all of these things. Catholic universities and colleges are complex, multifaceted endeavors, and faculty who cannot engage in these activities can still contribute in equally valuable ways to the mission of the university—as long as they do not undermine or obstruct the scholars who are engaged in these activities. Still, relying on merely the "extracurricular," "Catholic-values," or "theology-requirement" approaches to Catholic higher education will not be enough. If a critical mass of faculty in the social sciences is not doing the kinds of things suggested above, it is hard to see how their school can plausibly claim to be a Catholic university or college.

I do not intend the proposals above to apply only to the social sciences of Catholic universities and colleges. But as a social scientist, it seems wise to limit my arguments to the disciplines I know best. Other divisions of scientific and humanistic inquiry may require somewhat different approaches. The above also do not represent an exhaustive list of ideas, but only some of the practices that should characterize faculty, departments, and programs in the social sciences of a Catholic university or college. Some of them are more countercultural than others. But all must be understood, practiced, and rewarded by the administration and a critical mass of faculty at any university or college that intends to be *Catholic* not in name only but also in its intellectual inquiry, academic scholarship, and classroom teaching.

5

The Nearly Impossible
Balancing Act

*Achieving Undergraduate Excellence, Catholic
Education, and Premier Research University
Scholarship (Simultaneously)*

THE UNIVERSITY OF NOTRE Dame has adopted and committed itself, as I have noted repeatedly, to a three-part
mission. That mission is, in the words of President John
I. Jenkins, to "becom[e] a preeminent research university
with a distinctive Catholic mission and an unsurpassed
undergraduate education." I personally could not be more
enthusiastic about dedicating my efforts as a scholar,
teacher, and sometimes-administrator to helping Notre
Dame realize that mission. Every part of it inspires me
and directs my work. But the leaders of Notre Dame are
under no illusions about the difficulties they face in realizing this mission (as we saw in chapter 1). I myself have

grave doubts about our capacity to achieve it all, although I refuse to despair over the prospect.

The problem is not good intentions or even, in the case of Notre Dame, the material resources needed to fulfill the stated mission. The problem is the larger environment of American higher education and the constraints, expectations, and standards that it imposes on colleges and universities with ambitious visions. Leaders at Notre Dame have some (though certainly not absolute) control over what happens within our university's institutional bounds. They may even have some influence in what happens in American higher education more broadly. But, for the most part, higher education in the United States and beyond is an extremely complex institutional sector of a globalized world, operating with an immense momentum of cultural history and massive power to shape the specific people and schools that comprise it. That is what we sociologists call "the determining power of social structures over the individuals and organizations that emergently constitute them." Thus, if Notre Dame (or any other Catholic college or university) is interested in "playing ball" with everyone else on the field of American higher education, it has to play by rules that others make up and enforce, jump into the fray of other players' pushes and pulls, and generally subject itself to the myriad effects (intended or not) of every decision of every other player on the field.

In short, neither Notre Dame nor any other university can accomplish whatever it wants solely by committing itself to it and spending the necessary resources. The commitment and resources are, of course, *necessary* conditions for realizing a college's mission, but not *sufficient* conditions. Very many other intricate and powerful forces must also be negotiated. The big question, then, is whether Notre Dame can in fact negotiate them with adequate success to finally achieve the mission of "becoming a preeminent research university with a distinctive Catholic mission and an unsurpassed undergraduate education."

I very much hope so. But along the way, the more everyone involved understands the intricate and powerful forces, dynamics, and tendencies in higher education, the better we will know what we are up against and how to negotiate these factors more deftly. In the worst case, we may at least learn why we are losing ground or failing in some areas, and what alternative choices we might make to gain more accomplishments and face fewer disappointments.

Before proceeding, I must say that I do not consider myself an expert on these matters, insofar as I have not studied them systematically as a focus of my scholarship. However, I have spent half a century in schools at one level and sort or another, both religious and secular, both liberal arts– and research-oriented, in which I have played many roles—and to which in the last thirty years I have brought a sociological perspective to try to understand. I was educated at and, later, as a new professor, taught at a small liberal arts college in New England (Gordon College). I completed my graduate degrees (MA, PhD) at a major Ivy League school in the Northeast (Harvard University). I then worked for twelve years at a public, state research university in the South (the University of North Carolina at Chapel Hill). And for the last seven years, I have happily taught, researched, and served in various ways at the University of Notre Dame. So I have taught undergraduate students exclusively. And elsewhere I have trained numerous graduate students who are now successful faculty in sociology departments at universities and colleges around the country. I have conducted major, externally funded, social science research endeavors. I was the associate chair of a highly ranked sociology graduate (degree) and undergraduate (major) program. And I continue to teach Introduction to Sociology to first-semester freshmen students.

So I have seen higher education up close in a variety of settings: evangelical Protestant, secular private, secular public, and Catholic private settings. These experiences provide me with some insights into this chapter's central question: What are the tensions, trade-offs, and dangers involved in simultaneously seeking to sustain excellence in undergraduate education and remain a premier research university all in an institutional, cultural, and pedagogical context that is robustly Catholic?

Let us start with the most obvious and important factor: the kind of faculty a college needs to hire to achieve its mission. Faculty determine what can be achieved in any college or university, and they serve on the front lines with the students of any institution of higher education. The difficulty with Notre Dame's three-part mission is that it requires three different kinds of ideal faculty members for each of the three aspects of its mission. Achieving excellence in undergraduate, liberal arts education, for example, requires hiring faculty who are outstanding classroom teachers, who read and think broadly in a variety of fields, who love spending time with undergraduate students and having them over for dinner or cookouts, who provide extensive feedback on students' papers and exams, who want to organize field trips and service-learning education experiences, who agree to advise undergraduate honors projects and senior theses, most of which will not be published, who not only love big questions involving the life of the mind but also engaging eighteen- to twenty-two-year-olds in those questions, and who measure their career success by the kind of good, rich, happy, productive lives that their students go on to lead. Becoming great at those things typically (but not always) means sacrificing research, publishing, and staying on the cutting edge of developments in one's discipline and fields of interest.

By contrast, building a premier research university requires hiring faculty who are advanced specialists and authorities in their fields, who are dedicated to data collection and analysis, who know how to win generous research grants from funders and foundations, who measure success by the number of influential articles or books they can publish, who invest in presenting papers and networking with colleagues at conferences, and whose teaching is most focused on training promising graduate students to spread their influence in the discipline. Developing these traits usually (but not always) means prioritizing staying abreast of new developments in super-specialized fields, reducing undergraduate teaching loads as much as possible by "buying out of teaching" with grant money, devoting as much teaching as one can to graduate seminars, and spending discretionary time in labs and writing alone in one's office. While leading researchers and publishers are normally very smart people, they do not necessarily love eighteen- to twenty-two-year-olds and are not often oriented toward wrestling with big-picture intellectual questions.

What kind of faculty does a Catholic college or university need to accomplish Notre Dame's third mission of providing a rich Catholic environment and education? Such faculty must not only be well-grounded in their particular disciplines of study. They also need to be personally interested and broadly educated in the theological and philosophical issues related to the coherent integration of knowledge within an expansive Catholic framework. They need to be conversant with Church doctrines and moral and social teachings. They need to know enough about history and modernity to situate Catholic education within the larger contemporary reality. While they may question the Church's teachings on various issues, they ultimately should love the Church as loyal sons and daughters, offering any criticisms of it out of care for its well-being, not resentment and hostility. Such faculty need to exercise pastoral sensitivity in their relationship with students, caring for their personal and spiritual selves as well as their minds and careers. Ideally they participate regularly in campus Masses and are active members of their neighborhood parishes. As members of a Catholic community, they should model in their personal and family lives the kind of wholeness, integrity, and growth that the Catholic faith hopes to see in believers. They should also model reasonably Christian ways of dealing with their own brokenness and failures. They should be teachers and mentors who measure their career success through their contribution to the holistic formation of generations of students who graduate and become well-rounded Catholic adults who live their own lives well and faithfully. Best is having a minimum proportion of one's faculty be priests and religious sisters and brothers. Contributing in these ways to a school's Catholic mission often (but not always) means sacrificing the time and ability to maintain expertise in one's specialized fields, to attend all the professional meetings of one's discipline, to write research grant proposals, and to be a prolific publisher. There is one more professional pitfall to being such a faculty member: too close an identification with Catholicism can damage an academic's reputation as a legitimate scholar in his or her discipline.

Different kinds of faculty are also animated by different kinds of disciplinary questions and intellectual puzzles. Undergraduate teaching–oriented faculty generally like to read a wide variety of works—especially books—produced in their areas of interest and other works in areas beyond their disciplines that they find interesting. They tend to take a broader view of their disciplines in both appreciative and critical ways. Faculty who prioritize scholarly research tend to read more narrowly certain journals and books related to the specific fields in which they need to keep up and to which they want to contribute as publishing scholars. They usually focus on particular topics and puzzles on which they are contributing experts. Faculty devoted to furthering a college or university's Catholic mission are often similar to those dedicated to teaching undergraduates, only they also add readings in theology and perhaps philosophy, literature, ethics, and any other area that helps them sort out the big-picture issues they are attracted to analyzing. Their concern is less with disciplinary appreciation or research specialization than with intellectual integration and the cross-disciplinary synthesis of truth.

Finding scholars who fit all three of the profiles just described is nearly impossible. There are not enough people in the world with all of those diverse qualifications for the three types of faculty success. It is easier to find a faculty person with the skills both to provide undergraduates with an excellent liberal arts education and to foster a rich Catholic educational environment. Such faculty are by no means a dime a dozen, but they exist. They are the ones who make the best Catholic liberal arts colleges possible. Such scholars are tremendous assets to the Church and to Catholic higher education, and should be cultivated, appreciated, and rewarded.

But add to that combination the set of requirements needed in faculty who can build a premier research university, and the pool of candidates grows extremely thin. There simply are not that many faculty candidates out there who can contribute to all three aspects of the mission Notre Dame has set for itself. And even when such faculty can be recruited, inevitable constraints prevent them from fully developing all three sets of talents at the same time. The more they invest in undergraduate teaching, for example, the less time they have to put into remaining a top research scholar in their field—which disadvantages them relative to their colleagues at other schools who are happy to make teaching undergraduates a lower priority and do not care a hoot about Catholic formation and education. Furthermore, those few faculty who are unusually good on all three fronts tend to be highly visionary and capable at many other tasks, and so are often tapped for leadership positions in various centers, initiatives, institutes, and programs. Administrative burdens then squeeze out their contribution to undergraduate teaching, scholarly research and publishing, and Catholic intellectual life.

Given this structure of the situation, consider the following scenario. A Catholic college or university with our three-part mission discovers a faculty member at another school who is a serious Catholic intellectual, a very good teacher, and a quite good scholar. Should they hire him or her? More digging reveals that this person has published some very interesting and creative books with good university presses, but the books are off the beaten path relative to the mainstream concerns of the relevant discipline. He or she is a very good Catholic teacher, scholar, and intellectual, but not "a star." So should the Catholic college or university try to hire him or her? The budget only funds a limited number of faculty hires in any given year. If the college or university is trying to relatively quickly develop itself as a respected, even premier, research university, there are other faculty who could be hired instead who are younger and hotter in their fields and who would help achieve that goal more quickly. Unfortunately, most of them are not Catholic; others are non-practicing Catholics, who were baptized as infants but have fallen away from faith and do not think or live much like Catholics. Which among these candidates should be hired?

It would be possible—not easy, but with enough money, possible—to hire a department full of faculty who are among the best researchers and publishing scholars in their fields. But very many of them would be mediocre when it comes to undergraduate education and mostly deaf, dumb, and blind with regard to the Catholic intellectual life. It would also be possible to hire a department full of faculty who represent the most interesting, creative, and deep thinkers and teachers devoted to wrestling with matters of modern scholarship in light of the Catholic Church's intellectual and spiritual tradition. But they would almost certainly not do much to build their schools into leading research universities respected by their (mostly secular) peer institutions. And, thirdly, it would be possible to build academic departments with faculty who would provide undergraduate students with the very best liberal arts educational experience possible. But, similarly, they would almost certainly do little to advance the university's research, and may or may not know or care much about the Catholic mission. Which kind of faculty should a Catholic college or university with an ambitious three-part mission statement hire? And which should it choose to grant tenure to and promote after it has hired them and had some years to look them over?

The answer "some of each type" may seem to be a realistic compromise, but it brings problems of its own. A university would end up with faculty in each department with very different ideas of what they are doing, what students need, what counts as success, and how resources ought to be spent. The research-oriented faculty become frustrated with the "lack of productivity" of some their colleagues and with the odd Catholic trappings that others also want to emphasize. The teaching-oriented faculty become frustrated with the narrow focus of some of their colleagues on research, their lower-quality teaching, and their relative neglect of the undergraduate students; some of them may also think that the interest in Catholic mission among some colleagues is strange. And then those faculty who are invested in advancing the Catholic mission in their department become frustrated with the majority of their colleagues who do not understand or care about that. Hiring faculty of each type thus produces academic departments that are not coherent, whose faculty are frustrated, and that as a whole are not very successful at achieving any of the three aspects of the university's mission.

The difficulties involved in all of this are complicated by other factors related to institutional systems. In most disciplines, for example, to be at the forefront of scholarly research and publishing, faculty need to be relieved of teaching and win external research grants, which provide the requisite resources and time for researching and publishing at high levels. But that also removes those faculty from the classroom, devotes their attention to grant-writing and reporting, and reduces their ability to get to know undergraduate students. Some argue that what such faculty learn as active researchers benefits undergraduate students in the classroom over the long run, by stimulating the faculty members' minds and enabling them to expose students in the classroom to the latest research issues and processes in their disciplines. There is some truth to that. But I suspect that this argument is often oversold. More regularly, the faculty researcher's curriculum vitae grows and his or her undergraduate students lose. The necessary heavy emphasis on faculty grant-getting of aspiring research universities also transforms faculty cultures so that money and reducing one's class load become more prized than teaching, mentoring, and spending "quality time" with undergraduate students. Teaching sophomores becomes something faculty try to avoid rather than something they feel called to do. This transformation can happen subtly, but its institutional effects over time prove to be profound and are difficult, if not impossible, to reverse.

A large emphasis on research becomes institutionalized with fixed costs and bureaucracies as well. The need to win and process more and more external research funding brings with it the need for rapidly expanding Offices of Research, Grants Administration, Regulations Compliance, Accounting, and the other infrastructural and administrative offices that this work demands. In theory, these new costs are covered by the external research grant overhead and indirect funds. But it also influences the university's institutional culture—devaluing undergraduate education and Catholic intellectual life—and sends signals to prospective faculty, existing faculty, and students about the university's priorities.

Consider, for example, teaching replacements. When a regular faculty member wins an external grant that reduces his or her teaching load, how are the courses he or she would have otherwise taught now "covered"? Not generally by the institution hiring more tenure-track faculty. Rather, universities are powerfully tempted instead to hire more graduate student teachers and adjunct instructors, who are less expensive. Now, some such instructors can be excellent teachers of undergraduates. But many are not. Many graduate student instructors, for example, are using their teaching assignments as first-time practice in the classroom, as "teaching experiences" to add to their curriculum vitae, in which the undergraduate students serve as their pedagogical guinea pigs. An institution may justify this practice by noting that research universities also have the mission of producing good PhD scholar-teachers, which is true. But in the end, it is inevitably the undergraduate students who get the short end of the stick. And once the practice of replacing regular faculty in the classroom with graduate students and temporary adjuncts becomes established, it becomes very difficult to reverse.

Furthermore, faculty with external grant money and big research projects typically spend their summers working on their funded projects. That is when they have large blocks of time to devote to their research, and when they are usually able to pay themselves summer salaries from their research grants, which is attractive. That certainly enables faculty to become productive research scholars in their fields. But guess what then does *not* happen during their summers? Researchers are not catching up on the tall pile of readings on a range of interests to keep one's mind stimulated and sharp. They do not use their summers in part to rest and recover from an intense year of undergraduate teaching. Stepping back and thinking deep about big-picture matters related to life, school, and the world does not happen during summers, nor relearning a field and seriously revising a course syllabus and class lecture notes and presentations, nor taking undergraduate students on summer travel abroad programs or volunteer service trips. Such opportunity costs and trade-offs are impossible to measure and evaluate with standardized metrics, but they undoubtedly affect the quality of the undergraduate educational experience.

Consider, too, how the factors of academic status, prestige, and respect play into the questions at issue here. The big dogs in the world of American higher education are secular and mostly secularist institutions. Harvard, Princeton, Michigan, North Carolina, and Berkeley are the models to emulate. Catholicism for most people in such worlds is something between (at best) a quaint private belief system and set of traditional practices that some people for strange reasons hold onto, and (at worst) a pernicious, benighted, and oppressive hierarchy of power and oppression that should be destroyed. What the Catholic Church teaches about abortion, same-sex relationships, contraception, and other "hot button" political issues is outrageous and deeply offensive in most high-status institutions of higher education in America, where many ambitious Catholic colleges and universities wish to be accepted and respected. So these Catholic teachings are deeply embarrassing for many faculty at Catholic universities and colleges who care about the opinions of their not-so-Catholic colleagues. Many try to cover their embarrassment by highlighting Catholicism's emphasis on "peace and justice," but that only gets them so far.

I am confident that in my own discipline of sociology—which is, admittedly, particularly ideological and politicized—a huge swath of scholars would on principle never consider working at Notre Dame, merely because it is Catholic. Another large group of sociologists might be open to the possibility of working there, but would come to their job interviews with suspicions raised (partly in response to "warnings" from dissenting and disgruntled Notre Dame faculty) about its being Catholic. In sociology, as a result, we are disadvantaged in our capacity to hire the best sociologists on the market, who would help raise the formal rankings and informal academic respect granted to our department and program. Dealing with this disadvantage takes large amounts of identity work and preemptive damage control among our colleagues in the discipline, simply to have "Notre Dame" generate a neutral, rather than negative, response among those we might wish to hire and the mentors who advise them. And that normally involves working to downplay most of the distinctive characteristics of our Catholic university—except the "peace and justice" piece—to convince people that "we are really just like them" in the good secular schools.

Catholic university and college leaders, especially those with great financial resources, can be easily seduced by the allure of upward mobility, recognition, and acceptance in the status system of American higher education. American Catholics—who have for most of their history fought hard to be accepted as good, mainstream citizens in this traditionally very Protestant nation—may be especially vulnerable to becoming willing to pay the steep costs (decreasing their Catholic commitments) of entry into the club of acceptability in mainstream higher education. It is one thing, a good thing, for a Catholic college or university to wish to increase the quality of its education and research in order to be a better *Catholic* college and university. It is quite another thing, a bad thing, to make decisions and policies based on the desire to look more like one's secular peer institutions in order to win their respect and favor.

Great Catholic colleges and universities have to be great on their own terms, not by the standards of those who do not understand the rationale, purpose, and mission of Catholic higher education. Especially in this time of profound doubt about and reevaluation of the value and delivery of American higher education more generally, Catholic colleges and universities ought not to be groveling before or following the crowd, which is quite confused at present, but instead carving out new and better models for providing the best forms of education possible. Sometime down the road, the world may actually be grateful that Catholic colleges and universities had the confidence to blaze their own path rather than conform to everyone else's ideas of what higher education has to look like. Nobody changes the world by aping the world, as President John I. Jenkins noted in chapter 1 above. Change requires offering something different. Notre Dame has the potential to do that, but it must not become captive to the dominant values and standards of higher education.

But suppose that a Catholic college or university bites the bullet and commits itself decisively to making its Catholic mission a top priority. Making that happen is more easily said than done. One big reason is that almost none of the graduate school programs attended by prospective junior faculty do anything to prepare their students to think as Catholic intellectuals. If anything, most do a lot to undermine such thinking. So a college or university may interview a number of promising young scholars for various disciplines who are practicing Catholics and who in theory support the Catholic mission. But it cannot be assumed that most of those prospective faculty members have been formed theologically and philosophically in ways that enable them to advance the mission *intellectually* in their disciples, in ways I wrote about in the previous chapter. The dean may organize seminars, workshops, and other programs to bring these young faculty up to speed on such matters. But that inevitably consumes time, energy, and attention that their peers at other schools will be spending on researching, writing, and publishing. So asking young faculty to prepare themselves to contribute intellectually to their own school's Catholic mission has the unintended consequence of reducing their chances of success in tenure and promotion, and disadvantaging them as scholars relative to their peers who do not bear the "burden" of also being Catholic intellectuals. In other words, not only is it almost impossible to find faculty able to excel in teaching undergraduates, performing scholarly research, and advancing a school's Catholic mission, but it also puts those faculty relative to their peers at a disadvantage. So the conundrums are many.

All of these difficulties create many challenges and hard choices for leaders of Catholic colleges and universities. Should they hire a star scholar who is interested in joining them for some reasons, but who does not understand and may be resistant to the idea of the Catholic mission? Do they tenure and promote a junior faculty member who brings in a lot of outside research grant money, but who is sometimes a mediocre teacher in the classroom? Should they affirm and reward faculty who are keen critical thinkers about the relationship between their disciplines and Catholic faith, but who have become marginalized and arguably weak and outdated when it comes to the actual work of their disciplines? Such questions are myriad. The result of struggling with these questions may be great, but the difficulties involved at least match the value accomplished. I do not envy the dilemmas that face leaders of Catholic colleges and universities.

Returning to the concrete case of the University of Notre Dame, and the challenges its three-fold institutional mission involves, my own view is that the university can pursue all three goals, but that it must make priorities among them. Non-negotiables must be distinguished from ideal accomplishments. Constant commitments need to be differentiated from long-term aspirations. In my mind, Notre Dame ought to most highly prioritize two of its three mission goals, those on which it historically has already been strongest: excellence in undergraduate liberal arts education and achieving a distinctive Catholic identity, character, and education. The Catholic mission and the undergraduate mission are what made Notre Dame great and must always remain its "core business" that it never allows to slip but only continues to strengthen. That will undoubtedly mean having to be more patient and taking more time to develop itself as a great research university. So be it. Rome was not built in a day. And Catholics are more patient than most with long-term visions.

There are many great research universities in the world, and I hope Notre Dame will someday become one of them. But there is literally no other University of Notre Dame in the world, in the sense of that which has made Notre Dame outstanding. Notre Dame is unique in an almost invaluable way, in my view. And no amount of potential good that might be accomplished by quickly becoming a great research university, even a great Catholic research university, could offset the loss that process might entail in the university's ability to offer an excellent Catholic undergraduate liberal arts education. To lose the latter after more than a century and a half of envisioning and struggling to accomplish that mission would be a tragedy. Yet most of the sociological forces at work in higher education push the university toward just that outcome. So Notre Dame must take every move toward also becoming a premier research university with patient caution to protect all the good things that we already enjoy. That, I believe, is the disposition that leaders of Notre Dame must have if they are to honor its history and heritage, and to help it ultimately realize its greatest promise.

Conclusion

BUILDING CATHOLIC HIGHER EDUCATION in the United States today is a difficult, even countercultural endeavor. From the perspective of the Catholic faith, doing so makes complete sense. But within the larger culture and practices of contemporary American higher education, any seriously *Catholic* part of such an enterprise is confusing, if not frightening. Universities and colleges that are Catholic in "heritage," in extracurricular activities, in their "values" (at least certain of those that are acceptable), and even in requiring students to take theology courses are tolerable. But to be seriously Catholic when it comes to the heart of the mission and work of higher education is abnormal. Those who wish to build Catholic higher education today, therefore, confront many serious challenges and sometimes opposition—at times even from people within Catholic colleges and universities who do not understand or support the project. Catholic colleges that are content to operate largely within certain conservative sectors of American Catholicism face fewer of these problems, but arguably do so at the cost of parochial insularity (which is itself not very Catholic). The more Catholic colleges and universities seek to engage in mainstream disciplinary engagements and scholarly research and publishing, however, the more difficult become the challenges they have to negotiate. These problems cannot be ignored.

My own university, Notre Dame, is living through a crucial time of intently pursuing its stated three-fold mission of seeking to build upon and strengthen itself as a world-class institution in undergraduate education, scholarly research, *and* Catholic identity. That mission is ambitious, unique, and formidable. It is not clear whether we can succeed—or, if we only partly succeed, at what cost that partial success will come. Most worrisome to me is the question of whether excellence in undergraduate education and strong Catholic identity—the two areas in which Notre Dame already succeeds—will be inadvertently compromised for the sake of the status and money that come with success as a research university. American Catholics have always yearned for recognition and acceptance by the Protestant-dominated society to which they immigrated. And research money can—in fact, I think inevitably *does*—become an addictive stimulant to which universities become captive over time in ways that can distort their priorities and clarity of thought. It would not require anyone in authority at Notre Dame or elsewhere to intentionally let undergraduate education and Catholic identity decline. Enough powerful sociological forces are at work on their own in American higher education more broadly to corrode Notre Dame's commitments in these areas without any faculty and administrative negligence. Only the most attentive and determined efforts on the part of many leaders at Notre Dame in the administration and faculty will enable even the possibility of succeeding with its three-fold mission.

I have focused in this book especially on the implications of trying to build Catholic higher education for university and college *faculty*. Departmental faculty are ultimately those who determine whether undergraduate excellence is achieved, whether and how scholarly research gets conducted, and whether and how Catholic identity at the level of substantive intellectual engagement is worked out. Without the right kind of faculty in place, Catholic higher education will be crippled. *With* the right kind of faculty, however, Catholic higher education can thrive. So the right kind of faculty needs to be carefully recruited, cultivated, and built up over time. It is crucial, therefore, among other things, that everyone involved in Catholic higher education—from prospective faculty hires on up to university presidents—clearly understand institutional goals and expectations, and the many practical implications for faculty that logically flow from them. These matters are complicated, and how they are best worked out will vary from one Catholic college or university to another. I have tried in the chapters above to begin to spell out some of the implications for faculty as I see them. At the very least, such issues need to be openly discussed without fear and defensiveness. Clarity of vision, specificity, and confidence in mission and its implications are essential for Catholic colleges and universities to succeed in their appointed undertakings. To help advance matters in that direction at Notre Dame and in American Catholic higher education more broadly, this book is offered to clarify the issues at stake, promote constructive discussions, and identify the necessary decisions for successfully building Catholic higher education.

Appendix

The Role of Theology at a Catholic University

John C. Cavadini, University of Notre Dame,
Department of Theology

Why does Notre Dame require all undergraduate students to complete theology courses and why do other Catholic universities and colleges sometimes have similar requirements? What is theology, anyway? How does it benefit students? How does the university benefit from having a faculty of theology? What benefit, in return, does such a university offer the world of higher education? The presence of a theology department is unique to religiously affiliated colleges and universities, though certainly far from ubiquitous there, and even at Catholic schools these requirements have dwindled over the years, and often face challenges to justify themselves. What does it mean to accept a faculty of theology as an academic unit in a university community? Its presence implies something about the whole academic community because certain academic communities can and do exclude such departments.

Secular universities and colleges do not recognize theology as an academic discipline. The presence of a theology department, then, is not only a statement about the department itself, but about the academic community in which it is welcomed as a part. This Appendix hopes to suggest, in brief, some answers to the questions above, by drawing out what is implied, at least in a Catholic context, by the presence of a theology department, not as a separate divinity school, but as a unit within the college of Arts and Sciences or the equivalent, at a university.

We could begin by asking, then, what is distinctive about the academic community constituting a Catholic university? "By its very nature, each Catholic University makes an important contribution to the Church's work of evangelization. It is a living *institutional* witness to Christ and his message, so vitally important in cultures marked by secularism . . ." This passage from John Paul II's encyclical apostolic constitution *Ex Corde Ecclesiae* provides a characterization of the distinctiveness of a Catholic university.[17] It is, he says, a kind of "witness." This can sound somewhat startling, and I choose it, in part, for that reason. Witness is not a category that one finds applied to secular universities very often, if ever. At the same time it can seem puzzling to apply it to a university at all, though I imagine that even secular universities would count themselves as bearing witness in some way to values such as social justice, equality, and inclusiveness. According to *Ex Corde,* however, the witness of a Catholic university is connected to the Church's work of evangelization, and that seems to up the ante. A Catholic university, though proceeding "from the heart of the Church," is still not the same as the Church itself and its witness can't take the exact same form as in a parish or

17. John Paul II, *Ex Corde Ecclesiae: On Catholic Universities* (Washington, DC: US Conference of Catholic Bishops, 1996), 49.

a diocese. What then would that witness be, "so vitally important" as the pope says, "in cultures," such as our own, "marked by secularism"? Of course, this witness may take many forms in various activities in campus life, but here I am looking for the "institutional" witness, the witness that must be encoded into the very thing that makes a university a university, namely, its intellectual life, its mode of intellectual inquiry. Here, we find a crucial connection to theology as a discipline.

Theology is the "study of God" (*Theos-logos*). Wow! Studying God? That sounds weird and pretty subjective. After all, God seems mostly rather reclusive, not normally offering the divine self as an object of study. How could God be studied? How could one ever control such study, restraining it from becoming hopelessly subjective and fanciful? The study of God (*not* the same as the study of religion) sounds potentially like the study of an illusion of our own making. Unless, of course, one believes that God has in fact presented the divine self to us unto faith on our part. It is God's self-presentation, God's "revelation," that is the subject of theological study. Theology begins from faith in God's self-revelation and moves towards "understanding" what God has revealed. In that way, it is the study of God, or as Saint Anselm famously put it, "faith seeking understanding." Theology is the only discipline which has as its proper object God's revelation.

But, one could say, isn't revelation straightforward? Can't we just read it in the Bible and let it stop at that? Is there need for a special discipline to study it?

In the first place, for Catholics "revelation" is not only what is in Scripture, but is also contained in the apostolic "Tradition" of the Church. There was no New Testament around when Jesus lived, died, and rose. The Church preceded the New Testament and only gradually accepted its

writings as Scripture, just as the Jews preceded the Hebrew Bible, and only gradually ratified it as Scripture. The
Church's struggle over how and (even) whether to accept
the Hebrew Bible as Scripture was itself complex. There is
no book that dropped out of heaven with a self-verifying
label reading "FROM: God; TO: World; CONTENTS: Certified Inspired Scripture." Whether the book of Revelation
is Scripture was contested until the fifth century in some
Churches, and in fact Christians still disagree about what
constitutes inspired Scripture. Scripture is "the Church's
book," and Catholics have always valued the oral traditions
and the living liturgical practices in which Scripture was
used and came to be accepted as Scripture. Not every practice or homily is as valuable as every other, and the magiste-
rium of the Church, its teaching authority, is there to clarify
what is and what is not authentic Tradition as well as what
is or is not an acceptable interpretation of Scripture.

Studying God's self-revelation is therefore not
equivalent to studying Scripture. But even if it were, one
encounters problems in the scriptural texts, *quaestiones* or
"questions" as Saint Augustine called them in his sermons.
Many of these problems or questions are posed by the
learned disciplines, the arts and sciences, which one finds
at any university. To take a simple example, if according to
science, the sun does not move around the earth but the
earth around the sun, or the earth seems much older than
the 6,000 years or so the Bible envisions, then we have a
problem. Do we give up faith in revelation, or do we "seek
understanding"? Are we so sure we understand what Scripture is saying or how it is saying it?

Nor are these questions limited to the modern period.
Sophisticated intellectuals both Jewish and Christian have
for the past two millennia wondered about difficulties in
the book of Genesis: What kind of God creates supposedly

precious human creatures and then loses track of them in the garden, having to walk around calling out and asking where they are? For that matter, what kind of a God walks around in a garden at all? Nor does it take rocket science to notice that, in the first chapter of Genesis, light is created in verse 2, and "morning" and "evening" are mentioned, but the sun and the moon are not created until a few verses later. We moderns think we are the only ones burdened with such questions, but learned Jews and Christians of the first, second, and third centuries were possibly more troubled than we are by these passages, and yet they pressed on, "seeking understanding." What *was* the "day" created before the sun and the moon which define our days, and what was the "light" that preceded these heavenly bodies? Was it the light of created intelligence (the rational incorporeal spirit, not mentioned anywhere else in the narrative)? Was it the light of understanding, which pervades the text as a whole? Is God's creation of the first "day" a way of saying that God created time and that time is older than the sun and the moon?

No matter how they answered these particular questions, theologians of the early centuries agreed that the most important truths contained in these Scriptural texts were that the origin of the world is God's creative act and that creation is not simply a matter of mechanical origin but of God's "speaking." Creation is not just caused by God as the first mechanical cause among others, but in God's "Word" or intention, on which creation is completely dependent even after the first moment. Another crucial truth: that all that God created is good, indeed as a whole "very good," that the whole cosmos without remainder is good. And finally, that human beings have the special dignity of being created in the "image and likeness" of God. Have we yet fully understood the "goodness" of the cosmos and all that is in it? Do we understand fully what it means to be in the "image and likeness of God"? Of course not, but the "seeking" never stops because the questions never stop (for one thing). But now we have, besides the text of Scripture, the benefit of this tradition of consensus, built up from the earliest centuries, about the central meaning of these texts, and we can study that consensus, too, as we attempt to further our "understanding" in light of modern versions of the ancient questions: how *can* we square the texts of Genesis with what we understand from science?

We can do so primarily by noticing that the elements which the traditional consensus finds central—the origin and dependence of the world on God, the goodness of the world, and the dignity of human beings as God's "image and likeness"—are none of them measurable or empirically observable. In other words, this is not a scientific text at all, primitive or otherwise, and cannot in principle be replaced by one. Science cannot determine or measure the "goodness" of anything, no matter how sophisticated the instruments of detection. These are not statements proposed for scientific verification, but truths proclaimed unto faith, in the context of the rest of revelation, and one responds by faith and by seeking, in turn, to "understand" what one has come to believe, not by observing and testing and verifying the "hypothesis" of goodness, as would be appropriate for a scientific theorem based on empirical evidence. Faith in the goodness of creation proceeding from God's love is precisely that—faith. And if we are pressed by the obvious presence of evil in the world, that is grounds for working to understand further what is meant by the "goodness" we believe in, and how the doctrine of creation fits into the broader revelation of God's love.

Once we stop thinking of the text as some kind of primitive science, we might glimpse how self-consciously the text is proclaiming that its subject is a mystery too great for words. The six-day scheme is obviously a construct meant to underscore that very fact. No one can have observed even in principle the creative "speech" of God; isn't that the point of reserving the creation of the only possible observer until the sixth "day," when all the speaking is done? The fact that the structure of "days" precedes the creation of the sun and moon is the text's way of saying that this structure is a construct. The text announces, with this construct, that the mystery of which it is speaking is too great for words. The text thus makes itself a vessel containing the great light of a mystery that can shine through it, casting the very words of the text as its shadow. The creation story in Genesis is not a scientific account, primitive or otherwise, but announces itself as the bearer of a mystery that no science can prove, disprove, or even observe. It transcends scientific questions without in the least denying their validity. In fact, insofar as scientific results become questions that prompt a deeper understanding of the text, the results of science are affirmed, not denied.

It is worth pausing here. In this example, science is affirmed insofar as its results, fully accepted as scientific results, become questions pointing to something beyond science. Faith in revelation turns some results of science into questions that could not arise from or be answered by science, and so science itself becomes oriented towards an integration of knowledge that will occur on a level transcending science. One learns to recognize that some concepts, such as "creation," are irreducibly theological: they can't be reduced or translated into scientific categories because they arise from mysteries, such as the goodness of the cosmos, which are proclaimed to, and apprehended only by, faith. Language of "transcending" science is not meant as an insult to science, but only as a way of affirming it in its own methodology. A culture of "faith seeking understanding" is *not* a culture that holds that faith offers answers to scientific questions. It is *not* the position that there is a Catholic or Christian science and *not* a culture in which faith alone is regarded as a sufficient answer to all questions. The very point of theology is to engage the truths of faith in a "dialogue with reason," that is, with all the other disciplines that arise from the questioning of the human spirit and from observation of the world. Theology affirms the truths of other disciplines even as it integrates them into a realm of discourse that transcends their methodologies and results. This theological discourse generates a kind of thick intellectual culture, shot through at once with mystery and with reason, with irreducible mystery always in the lead, shining beneath and giving the culture its shape, even as that culture takes on life in its puzzling over the results of all other disciplinary research.

Nor does this apply only to the natural sciences. If anthropological research into other cultures of the world discovers religious teachings of undeniable and exquisite beauty, these results are left standing on the one hand, but precisely as results, also become questions: how can we understand their truth relative to revelation? "Faith seeking understanding" can afford to acknowledge truth wherever it may be found without fearing that God's self-revelation in Christ is somehow threatened. It cannot be threatened by truth. "Seeking" in this case means to deepen our own "understanding" of revelation even as we deepen our own thinking about other religions.

Now we can see why a university community that accepts in its midst a theology department is not different simply because it accepts one more discipline than secular universities do. In accepting that discipline, a university is not just adding another element to the paradigm already in place at secular universities but *actually accepting a whole different paradigm of the intellectual life, a paradigm of intellectual culture as a dialectic between faith and reason,* to use the traditional expression. Having a theology department means accepting a commitment to the intellectual life as oriented towards an "understanding" of something *transcending all the disciplines.* The *openness to that transcendent mystery,* beyond all of the disciplines, affirms them all but keeps each one from closing in on itself as though the truths it discovered were incommensurable with the truths discovered by other disciplines. It means openness to a conversation that necessarily transcends each discipline but is not merely "interdisciplinary." If the disciplines converge at some point, it must be at a point "above" them all, in a discipline that has as its explicit object of study the mystery that transcends all other objects of study. Otherwise one must either force non-disciplinary solutions onto the disciplines (for example, offering faith as an adequate scientific answer) or declare that knowledge is necessarily shattered into shards of truth that are absolutely incommensurate with each other. For an academic community, *accepting theology as an academic discipline means an openness to the idea of an integration of knowledge,* and it means having the possibility of succeeding, because in order to be truly integrative and not just interdisciplinary the conversation at some point necessarily becomes theological.

The task of seeking an integration of knowledge has been called a "sapiential task,"[18] "sapiential" because it is a "search for the ultimate and overarching meaning of life," i.e., wisdom. In other words, the Catholic intellectual life is inescapably not something finished and settled or even potentially so, but *a quest,* as John Paul II says in another

18. John Paul II, *Fides et Ratio: On the Relationship of Faith and Reason* (Boston: Pauline, 1998), 85.

place: "Integration of knowledge is a process, one which will always remain incomplete."[19] This quest *verges towards* wisdom, and as a whole the Catholic intellectual life in its open-endedness can be thought of as a wisdom tradition. It is inescapably theological because it grows out of faith in the God of revelation, and theology performs the essential integrative function. Traditionally philosophy has been (and still is) a disciplinary partner in the integration of the intellectual life, since it asks questions that in fact transcend the disciplines, "meta-questions" proper to the nature of knowledge itself, for instance, or of language, or of meaning, and even, as Saint Thomas points out, of God. Still, philosophy does not in the end have as its defining object of study God's self-revelation and everything as seen in the light of God's self-revelation, as Thomas also points out in the first article of the *Summa Theologiae*. Philosophy can remain philosophy without asking the question of the relation of its own results to revelation, and if the question is asked, it cannot be answered without theology. Further, contemporary philosophy often does not even concern itself with questions of transcendence or ultimate meaning, and it remains philosophy without doing so. But if theology ceases to address itself to God's self-revelation, it ceases to be theology.

Yet theology achieves no "understanding" apart from the other disciplines (because "reason discovers new and unsuspected horizons," because "faith and reason mutually support each other; each influences the other, as they offer to each other a purifying critique and a stimulus to pursue the search for deeper understanding").[20] *Thus, the Catholic intellectual life, as a theologically integrated wisdom tradition, provides a middle ground between secularism and*

19. John Paul II, *Ex Corde Ecclesiae*, 16.
20. John Paul II, *Fides et Ratio*, 73, 100.

sectarianism. This is the "witness," specific to a *university*, that a *Catholic* university can—and does—provide in our culture.

What benefit does this witness offer to the American academy in general? Without this witness, the academic imagination in our country will remain dominated by and limited to the increasingly sterile polarity between aggressive secularization on the one hand, and aggressive anti-intellectual fideisms on the other. These are equally unattractive inverse mirror images of each other, and each serves to perpetuate the other. Seven years ago, Stephen Pinker famously observed that "universities are about reason, pure and simple," and that "faith—believing something without good reasons to do so—has no place in anything but a religious institution," by which he meant a church, synagogue, mosque, or the like.[21] Such a caricature of faith is itself anti-intellectual, but, insofar as persons of faith can be repelled by a secularizing momentum so aggressive it seeks to remove perspectives of faith from the curriculum, they can be tempted to turn to a kind of isolationist, fideistic, or fundamentalist position that finds in faith an intellectual world sufficient to itself. But such cultures are usually so narrow, even anti-intellectual, that they prompt a kind of intellectual revulsion, and so feed the growth of the opposite pole—secularization, which at least seems open to all questions (if not all answers!). There has to be an alternative that offers hope for a different kind of solution, and that is the "witness" that a Catholic university is called upon to provide. One could almost call this mission a healing of intellectual imagination, stymied and bound by the cultural polarity of secularism and sectarianism.

21. Stephen Pinker, "Less Faith, More Reason," *Harvard Crimson,* October 27, 2006.

Appendix

It should be noted that this witness will "pinch" a little on both sides of the intellectual equation. It will "pinch" on the "understanding" side of the equation "faith seeking understanding" because a witness must be specific to some commitment, in this case, to faith in God's self-revelation as entrusted to the Church. This requires links to the Church. Without these links, the intellectual culture of the university will, beyond any doubt, be secularized. Apart from the Church, the community of believers, there is no one who cares enough about it. In a way, the Church protects this intellectual environment. On the other hand, the dialectic between faith and reason toward understanding has to be unconstrained enough so that real thinking is possible, and so to some it will seem to "pinch" on the "faith" side of the equation. Academic credibility is a *sine qua non* if any witness appropriate *to a university* is to be borne; fidelity is a *sine qua non* if any *distinctive* intellectual culture is to offer any witness. The question here would be, are the connections to the Church accidental and occasional or programmatic and consistent? Is the programming *rooted in* ecclesial contexts and *linked to* ecclesial persons and *accountable* in some way to authority in the Church? Is dissent the default mode defining the theological culture? Or is refusal to tolerate public questioning of various magisterial positions the default mode? If either is the case, you probably are not striking the right balance.

Now we are in a position to answer the remaining questions we set for ourselves at the beginning of this Appendix. Why should undergraduates be required to take courses in theology? An undergraduate course in theology is essentially different from, say, an undergraduate course in history. Even in cases where some texts would be shared in common, the point of a history course is to find out about these texts or their historical contexts: the circumstances of their production, the culture behind them, the historical situation for which they provide evidence. But the point of a theology course is to find out about God, in and through the properly disciplined study of these texts. If a student asks a question about God in a history class, the instructor is not violating disciplinary identity to say "that's not a relevant question in this class" (or, as it was said to me somewhat indecorously in a class at my non-Catholic undergraduate institution, "Please leave your theological baggage at the door"). But should a theology instructor reply in the same way, he or she would violate the very identity of the discipline. Students are right to ask about God, and all matters related to God, in a theology class, because the issue is not finally "What influences were operating in Julian of Norwich's social setting that caused her to have visions?" or "What did Thomas Aquinas think about God?"—though questions like these are certainly involved—but rather, "How has this study helped *me* think about God and God's self-revelation?"

From theology classes, students also can learn that faith in revelation is not something that must remain a private matter, an individualistic affair of piety without reference to the intellectual life, but rather can be as sophisticated as that of any other discipline of study in the university—yes, the very same faith that their less educated friends and relatives also turn to for challenge and consolation. I find that this is the single most important benefit of the study of theology for undergraduates, namely, discovery of the hitherto (for them) unsuspected sophistication of the "science of God," of the perspective of faith—it comes as a shock almost. If anything is likely to bind them more fully to their faith, it is this discovery, not, in the first instance, intellectually unchallenging courses that seem merely to be preaching to them. I say "merely" not because I want to devalue preaching, but because I want to emphasize the context of a university. The witness of a university is not the same as that of a parish or a diocese where preaching is the *modus operandi*.

Through required courses in theology, students are exposed to a mode of inquiry that exposes the fallacy of the dichotomy between secularization and sectarianism, where faith is not excluded as irrelevant to reason but where faith itself seeks understanding, where faith itself is the opening to a rich intellectual world. The *initium fidei*, the "starting point of faith" as Augustine calls it, drives this inquiry, rather than cuts it short. Nor are we talking about "faith" as a general attitude, or faith in the abstract, but a specific faith, a specific starting point, the basic doctrines or mysteries of the Catholic faith, considered as part of a living tradition and not an artifact of the past. The basic knowledge gained offers a benefit to any student of Western culture, believing or not, and the same is true for training in a mode of inquiry that refuses to oppose faith and reason (the common underlying position of both secularism and fideism) while yet refusing to reduce faith to reason.

As students come to understand the sophistication of the Catholic theological tradition, I find that their sympathy for it increases. They see riches where before they saw old, irrelevant texts. They come to appreciate that there were difficult challenges in the Church before, controversies that make some of those we experience today pale by comparison. They discover a beauty they had not expected, find out that Scripture is not as "primitive" as they had thought, discover variety where previously they had thought only of uniformity. They learn that, without being reducible to reason, faith has a rationality about it that makes belief seem reasonable even if never provable. They learn some of the basic doctrines of the Catholic faith, not as doors that close off reflection, but as doors that open into lifelong reflection on the ultimately ineffable mystery of God's love, the ultimate referent of all doctrine. It is the formation of an intellectual life, both in the individual and in the academic culture at large, which is a continuing engagement with this mystery, that is the principle benefit of theology as a field of study for undergraduates and for all.

Thus the Catholic university that welcomes a theology department in its academic midst, and requires theology courses, endorses an intellectual approach that is intrinsically *integrative*. Even without any specific integrating programming, the university thereby identifies its whole intellectual modality as distinctive, one that is potentially integrative without being homogenizing. The disciplines remain themselves, and distinctive disciplinary methodologies are not erased or collapsed into each other, but each disciplinary conversation is experienced *ipso facto* as part of a larger whole. Since one part of it, endorsed as a requirement, is explicitly oriented towards "understanding" the mystery of God's self-revelation, the whole is thereby implicitly oriented towards such understanding. The conversation tends towards an integration that is never complete but always a work in progress, which, as an orientation towards integration already *is*, to some extent, integration.

Perhaps a small concrete example might be proposed to illustrate what programming might look like where the integrative orientation of the conversation becomes more actualized. Contrary to popular belief, the "preferential option for the poor" is first and foremost a doctrine about God, and not about the poor: "The ultimate basis of God's preference for the poor is to be found in God's own goodness and not in any analysis of society or in human compassion, however pertinent these reasons may be."[22] If the

22. Gustavo Gutiérrez, *On Job: God-Talk and the Suffering of the*

poor and the "little ones" are "the privileged addressees of revelation," this is "the result not primarily of moral or spiritual dispositions, but of a human situation in which God undertakes self-revelation by acting and overturning values and criteria. The scorned of this world are those whom the God of love prefers."[23] All good universities want to be committed to social service of some kind, and the Catholic university most of all. But it is important to note here that from a Catholic point of view, the reason is first and foremost based in *God's* manner of self-revelation. We are, in the first place, confronted with a mystery of God's transcendent love that cannot be reduced to human reason, because it is a "preference," based in God's "goodness." It cannot be derived from any notion of "justice" based on human reason alone, on the supposed merits or lack of merits exhibited by the poor. Theology, then, inescapably becomes at very least a contemplative discourse that is defined by an attempt to "understand" this goodness, and to arrive at a notion of justice which flows from it. The language appropriate to theology at this juncture, according to Gutiérrez, is the union of the contemplative and prophetic, of the contemplation of God's love and the "overturning" it implies in its very mode of revelation. Wouldn't this language, which must arise and can only arise in a department oriented by definition to the Mystery of God's self-revelation, offer one possible enactment of the "integration" required of a Catholic university, as the various disciplines contribute to the "language" of contemplation and of justice, to the terms of its "understanding" in this world of science, technology, law, literature, and social studies? There could even be clusters of linked courses, each of which speaks its own disciplinary language, but as linked together, can be integrated

Innocent (Maryknoll, NY: Orbis, 1987), xiii.

23. Ibid.

theologically into the language of "contemplation" and "prophecy." And so, by mere presence and acceptance of a theology department, and a deepened reflection on what that means, we find ourselves, across the curriculum, almost unexpectedly oriented toward transcendent mystery. In particular, we find ourselves oriented toward the mystery in which these two languages, of love and justice find themselves united, as Gutiérrez puts it, in the language of God's solidarity with the "little ones," namely, the language of the Cross. Is there a better way to prepare students for a lifetime of active, conscious immersion in the mystery of God's love?